# Studies in FIRST CORINTHIANS

MESSAGES ON PRACTICAL CHRISTIAN LIVING

## M.R.DeHaan, M.D.

Lamplighter Books Grand Rapids, Michigan
Zondervan Publishing House

*Lamplighter Books* are published by Zondervan Publishing House, 1415 Lake Drive, S.E., Grand Rapids, Michigan 49506

STUDIES IN FIRST CORINTHIANS
Copyright 1956 by Zondervan Publishing House
Grand Rapids, Michigan

*Assigned to Dr. M. R. DeHaan, 1966*

ISBN 0-310-23311-9

*Printed in the United States of America*

84  85  86  87  88 — 30  29  28  27  26  25  24  23

# FOREWORD

This volume on First Corinthians is not an exhaustive exposition of this unusual epistle. No attempt has been made to cover its contents in a verse by verse exposition, and many passages are passed over without comment. An exhaustive treatise would require many volumes. Instead, only the most important problems are discussed with especial emphasis on the subjects which are of present-day interest and application.

The church at Corinth was a "problem" church. Some of these problems are discussed in this volume. These were chosen from among others because of their importance in the life of the believer. Most of the passages which have not been dealt with are explanations and applications of the particular problem dealt with.

We trust and pray that the material in this volume may serve as an incentive to the reader for a more thorough study of the entire epistle. The need today is for a "practical faith" which works in the lives of Christians, and I know of no more valuable exercise in the attainment of this end than the teaching of First Corinthians.

M. R. De Haan

*Grand Rapids, Michigan*

# INTRODUCTION

PAUL'S letters to the Corinthians (I and II Corinthians) are unique among the epistles of the apostle of grace. There is little similarity between them and his other epistles. First Corinthians was written in response to serious rumors concerning the spiritual state of the Corinthian church (Chapter 1:11). Moreover, Paul had received a letter from the church seeking his counsel with regard to certain serious differences of opinion among the members of the assembly (Chapter 7:1). It was to correct these errors that the epistle was written. First Corinthians (unlike Paul's other epistles) contains a minimum of doctrinal teaching. The Corinthians were spiritual "babies," immature and undeveloped, and unable to endure heavy doctrine, and so Paul feeds them on milk (Chapter 3:1,2).

The Corinthian church was a carnal church. Many of its members were but recently converted from paganism and found it difficult to separate themselves from their old life. As a result the epistle is largely corrective and exhortatory, rather than doctrinal. Paul severely condemns their carnal practices and childish sectarianism. However, the letter does contain some solid doctrinal meat. Chapter 15 on the Resurrection of the Body is the most complete doctrinal discussion of that subject in the Scriptures.

Another point of distinction was the abundance of special gifts which God gave to the Corinthian church. Among these were the gifts of prophecy, working of miracles, discerning of spirits, divers kinds of tongues, and the interpretation of tongues. All these gifts were peculiar to this carnal, worldly church. They were not found in the other churches in the measure they were in this carnal, immature church. These gifts belonged to the infancy of the church, and the "childhood days" of believers (I Corinthians 14:20; 13:11).

The gift of tongues is not mentioned in the other epistles of Paul. They were a sign of immaturity and spiritual "childishness." Paul does not endorse the Corinthians' abuse of these gifts, but rather condemns their unscriptural use and then lays down some specific rules, which, if followed, would end all the confusion about this vexing problem.

There is an abundance of practical instruction in the epistle, which the Church has overlooked for ages, and we pray that these simple studies may cause many to be revived, instructed and corrected. Paul deals with the matter of discipline (Chapter 5), going to law (Chapter 6), marriage and divorce (Chapter 7), Christian liberty (Chapters 8, 9, 10), and abuses at the Lord's Table (Chapter 11). The section on "tongues" covers three chapters (12 to 14), and the resurrection, one chapter (Chapter 15).

May the Lord bless the study of these much-ignored and neglected truths to the reader, and cause us to "grow up" into spiritual maturity and fruitfulness.

This volume should be read with the open Bible beside you. To obtain the greatest blessing, you should first read the entire epistle carefully and prayerfully. In the assurance of God's blessing upon His Word (Isaiah 55:10, 11) we send forth this volume to the glory of God.

# CONTENTS

*Chapter One*

# THE CARNAL CHURCH

> Now I beseech you, brethren, by the name of our Lord
> Jesus Christ, that ye all speak the same thing, and that there
> be no divisions among you; but that ye be perfectly joined
> together in the same mind and in the same judgment (I Co-
> rinthians 1:10).

THIS is the apostle Paul's impassioned plea and severe rebuke to the members of the assembly of the church in Corinth.
In this verse he gives us the occasion and the purpose for
the writing of this important epistle, so much neglected and
misunderstood by believers. It also gives us the answer
to the tragic carnality in the Corinthian church, which called
for the rebuke of Paul. He pleads for unity and co-operation,
and for a growth in grace in the knowledge of the Lord
Jesus Christ, that they may become mature and progress from
their present, immature, imperfect state of spiritual development and infancy.

### Occasion For Epistle

To understand the occasion and the purpose of this epistle,
we must review briefly the history of the church in Corinth.
Paul had visited the city of Corinth on his second missionary
journey. After a most discouraging experience in Athens
(Acts 17:15-34), Paul goes on to Corinth, greatly de-
pressed in spirit, and here again meets with unusual opposition.
He would have abandoned the city entirely, and gone on to
Ephesus except for a special revelation of encouragement
which he received from the Lord. In Acts 18 we are told
that after Paul had turned away from the synagogue in

9

disappointment, he had been compelled to conduct his meetings in a private home. Here is the record:

> And he [Paul] departed thence [from the synagogue], and entered into a certain man's house, named Justus, one that worshipped God, whose house joined hard to the synagogue (Acts 18:7).

This must have been a tremendously humiliating experience for the apostle Paul, to be cast out as it were from the church, thrown out of the synagogue, and rejected by organized religion. He is now compelled to hold meetings in a house. Undoubtedly his enemies took this as a sign of defeat, and it greatly troubled Paul. The record seems to suggest that this greatly discouraged him, and he was ready to give up in Corinth, for verse nine continues:

> Then spake the Lord to Paul in the night by a vision, Be not afraid, but speak, and hold not thy peace:
> For I am with thee, and no man shall set on thee to hurt thee: for I have much people in this city.
> And he continued there a year and six months, teaching the word of God among them (Acts 18:9-11).

It is interesting to note how, when Paul is rejected by the religionists in the synagogue and compelled to hold meetings in a private home, that it is only then that the Lord appears to Paul in a revelation. It reminds us of the blind man in John 9, who also was cast out of the synagogue, and then Jesus found him. This experience has been a common one among true and faithful servants of the Lord, that when they were rejected by men, then it was that the Lord gave them special power and unction, and began to bless their ministry. It is when we are willing to be rejected of men, and to take our place outside the camp, that our Lord often comes to His own, and the place of separation becomes the place of blessing. To be rejected of men is often a sign of acceptance with the Lord. The Lord Jesus Christ Himself said:

> Woe unto you, when all men shall speak well of you (Luke 6:26).

And again, He said:
> Blessed are ye, when men shall revile you, and persecute
> you, and shall say all manner of evil against you falsely, for
> my sake.
> Rejoice, and be exceeding glad: for great is your reward
> in heaven (Matthew 5:11, 12).

## A Long Ministry

And so Paul found that when he was where God wanted
him, no matter how difficult the position might be, he was
in the place of blessing. For he continued in Corinth for
eighteen months, and great numbers were saved. The church
in Corinth became a large church, for God said to Paul, "I
have much people in this city" (Acts 18:10b).

Then after a year and a half, Paul departs and moves on
to the city of Ephesus. A few years go by, and Paul makes
his second visit to Ephesus, and from there writes this
letter to the Corinthian church. The occasion for writing
was a discouraging and distracting rumor which came to him
from Corinth concerning the spiritual state of the church
where he had labored so faithfully and so earnestly for a
year and a half. Paul mentions this report in Chapter 1:
> For it hath been declared unto me of you, my brethren,
> by them which are of the house of Chloe, that there are con-
> tentions among you (I Corinthians 1:11).

The church at Corinth was being divided into cliques or
sects. Some followed Paul others clung to Apollos, while
others found Peter as their idol, and a few "holier-than-thou"
individuals said, "We do not follow men, but Christ." And
they said, "We are of Christ." This report of the condition
in Corinth was undoubtedly the reason for Paul's writing
this epistle in an effort to correct the evil of carnality and
incipient sectarianism in the church. Another reason for
writing this epistle seems to have been a letter to him at
Ephesus from the church at Corinth itself, concerning certain controversial questions, such as marriage and Christian
liberty, going to law with one another, and especially the

matter of the confusion of speaking in tongues, and certain errors concerning the resurrection.

And so Paul answers this letter concerning these various problems, but also makes it the occasion for dealing with a number of other even more serious conditions which prevailed in the church. This, then, is the setting and the occasion for this first epistle to the church at Corinth.

## Nature of the Epistle

This letter to Corinth, therefore, is unique among the letters of Paul. It is unlike any of the other epistles which are recorded for us in the Scriptures. Together with II Corinthians, it is quite different from anything that Paul ever wrote. The Corinthian epistle contains a minimum of doctrine. This sets it apart from all the other epistles. It is almost completely occupied with Christian conduct and behavior. While it does contain some doctrinal teaching, as we shall see, it is predominately practical and exhortatory and for the purpose of correcting certain errors and evils in the church. On the other hand, almost all of the other epistles of Paul follow a different and definite pattern in structure. In the other epistles of Paul, the first part is always given over to doctrinal teaching, and then the last part makes the practical application of the doctrine to the reader's everyday life. But in I Corinthians, Paul gives very little doctrine; immediately he plunges into the practical exhortations of correction and censure and instruction.

## Carnal Church

The reason for this Paul also gives in chapter 3, verses 1 to 3:

> And I, brethren, could not speak unto you as unto spiritual, but as unto carnal, even as unto babes in Christ.
>
> I have fed you with milk, and not with meat: for hitherto ye were not able to bear it, neither yet now are ye able.
>
> For ye are yet carnal: for whereas there is among you envying, and strife, and divisions, are ye not carnal, and walk as men? (I Corinthians 3:1-3).

## Milk For Babies

This epistle, therefore, may appropriately be called "Milk for Babies." The Corinthian believers were "babes in Christ," underdeveloped, undernourished, suffering from malnutrition, contentious, quibbling, fighting, criticizing, and acting like little children, looking for childish things such as signs and wonders, and seeking for miracles and tongues and manifestations, and other evidences which belong to the spiritual immaturity of the child of God, and are not for the mature Christian believer. Paul calls them *carnal*. The word "carnal" is a translation of the word "sarx," in the Greek, and means "flesh," and refers to the old nature received by our first birth. While these Corinthians were saved, and had been justified by faith, and are, therefore, addressed as "brethren" by Paul, they were, nevertheless, still unseparated from the flesh and the things of the world. The old nature was still predominant in their lives, as manifested by their conduct and behavior. Hence Paul says they "walk as men."

Now it is to correct this situation that Paul writes this epistle. It is largely a condemnatory epistle, for he condemns their fleshly behavior, and in love seeks to correct them and show them a more excellent way. The epistle is, therefore, we repeat, "milk for babies."

In our coming messages we shall take up the various problems which Paul discusses. But before we close this introductory message, we would like to leave one cardinal lesson with you. It is the warning against following men instead of Christ. The church in Corinth was divided into four distinct groups or cliques — those who saw and admired only Paul; others who followed the eloquent Apollos; still others who clung to the apostle Peter; and then those who piously asserted, "We are of Christ."

In this situation in the Corinthian church, therefore, we find all the seeds of incipient sectarianism and denominationalism, because the members had their eyes on men, and were enamored by the personalities of the servants of God, instead of keeping their eyes fixed on the person of the Lord Jesus Christ. They were more interested in dogma and pet doctrines and hairsplitting than in worshiping the Lord. The error of carnality as seen in this first epistle to the Corinthians has plagued the Church until this very day. The multiplicity of sects and divisions and denominations built upon some petty, hairsplitting doctrine or insignificant difference of ritual or ceremony must indeed be displeasing to the Lord. How much of the division in Christianity has come because Christians have followed certain striking personalities and men with whom they became enamored, instead of the Lord Jesus. Following a human personality instead of following the head, Christ, is one of the great reasons for the divisions among born-again believers which have sapped the power and the testimony of the Church, and have enervated the ministry of the Church by duplication, overlapping, quibbling and wrangling over nonessentials. In their divisions, Christians have forgotten that the fruit of the Spirit is love, joy and peace. And the world recognizes this inconsistency. The world refuses to believe our testimony and our message of Christ, because it sees so little of Christ in us. The world forms its estimate of the Lord Jesus only from observing those who claim to be His followers. May the Lord, therefore, teach us through these messages to be more like Him, to get our eyes off circumstances and things, self, the world, and men, and then to be occupied only with Him who,

> when he was reviled, reviled not again; when he suffered, he threatened not; but committed himself to him that judgeth righteously:
> . . . by whose stripes ye were healed (I Peter 2:23, 24).

## Chapter Two

# GOD IS FAITHFUL

> For it hath been declared unto me of you, my brethren, by them which are of the house of Chloe, that there are contentions among you.
>
> Now this I say, that every one of you saith, I am of Paul; and I of Apollos; and I of Cephas; and I of Christ.
>
> Is Christ divided? was Paul crucified for you? or were ye baptized in the name of Paul? (I Corinthians 1:11-13).

THE church at Corinth was split into factions, cliques and sects, and the result was envy, strife, contention and division. The church at Corinth was the typical carnal church, a congregation of spiritual babies, undernourished, spiritual cry babies, selfish and fleshly in their conduct.

Paul was so deeply concerned over this condition which had been called to his attention by a certain family in Corinth, as well as by a letter from the church itself, that he writes this rather lengthy epistle of rebuke and correction. The first thing we are to remember, however, is that these people to whom Paul wrote were true, born-again believers. Surely one would not gather this from their behavior, but Paul recognizes the fact that they were saved by grace, and by grace alone. Even though they were carnal and fleshly and far from perfect, they were nevertheless saved by the grace of God. This is the first thing which Paul seems to emphasize in this epistle. Before dealing rather sharply with the evils in the assembly, he reminds them of their relationship to Christ, and their position in Christ, and makes this very fact, that they are saved and kept by the grace of God, the basis and plea and argument for their repentance.

This is graphically seen in the introduction to this epistle. To this we must give some attention in order to understand what Paul is dealing with. Notice, therefore, the opening verses:

> Paul, called to be an apostle of Jesus Christ through the will of God, and Sosthenes our brother,
>
> Unto the church of God which is at Corinth, to them that are sanctified in Christ Jesus, called to be saints, with all that in every place call upon the name of Jesus Christ our Lord, both their's and our's (I Corinthians 1:1, 2).

## CALLED SAINTS

After Paul declares in the opening sentence his apostolic authority, as received from God and God alone, and not ordained by men, he addresses the members of the Corinthian church. Notice that he says three things:

1. He calls them the "Church of God."
2. He calls them "sanctified" in Christ Jesus.
3. He calls them "saints."

We emphasize this opening statement of Paul to this worldly, sectarian, carnal church. No other church was so full of evil and carnality, divisions and spiritual pride, so given to the works of the flesh, as this church. Yet Paul calls them "the church of God," "sanctified in Christ Jesus," and he calls them "saints." Looking at the church with its divisions, envying, strife and worldliness, and all of its faults, many would be ready to say, "They are not Christians at all. They have never been born again." But Paul knew better. He knew that salvation does not depend upon works, but on grace; not on our behavior, but on the love and provision of a sovereign God. If these Corinthians were to be justified and saved by their own goodness and by their conduct or behavior, surely there would be no hope for them at all. And that is true of all of us — of every single believer. If we were to be judged by our own merits and by our own worth and our behavior, in this world, it would be hopeless, for God demands perfection and nothing less than perfection. But we are not only saved by grace, but kept by grace as well.

## Saved By Grace

God knew, therefore, before He saved you what a failure you would be after you were saved. Yes, God foreknew what a mess we would all be prone to be, even after we were saved, and, therefore, He made adequate provision for us. So, too, it was with the Corinthians. If we were to judge them by their conduct and behavior, by the law and its demands, we might readily doubt their salvation; but Paul knew that they had been saved by the grace of God, and so he pleads with them on the basis of this grace to turn from their error, and their carnality and worldliness. He does not threaten them with losing their salvation, or scare them into obedience by telling them that they have lost their position in Christ. He does not wield the club of the law over their heads. Instead, he reminds them of God's faithfulness and grace, and makes the fact that God still holds on to them, the plea for repentance and the basis for their giving up all their sins.

## Grace and Peace

No wonder then that verse 3 begins with "grace," and he says:

> Grace be unto you, and peace, from God our Father, and from our Lord Jesus Christ (I Corinthians 1:3).

And then will you notice very carefully the following verse, verse 4:

> I thank my God always on your behalf, for the GRACE OF GOD which is given you by Jesus Christ (I Corinthians 1:4).

He does not say, "I thank God for your faithfulness and your good behavior." He does not say, "I thank God that you are such nice people." Ah, no! Paul couldn't do that, but he says instead:

> I thank my God always on your behalf, for the GRACE OF GOD.

On their own merit and their own worth these Corinthians would all be hopelessly lost, but the grace of God on their behalf is their only security. And notice that this grace is not earned, but it is GIVEN by Jesus Christ. It is all of grace, or none would be saved.

Paul goes on in this emphasis on the grace of God, and says,

> I thank my God . . . that in every thing ye are enriched BY HIM, in all utterance, and in all knowledge;
> Even as the testimony of Christ was confirmed IN YOU:
> So that ye come behind in no gift; waiting for the coming of our Lord Jesus Christ (I Corinthians 1:5-7).

We are to notice very carefully in this passage that it is *all* of God, and, therefore, it is *all* of grace. They were enriched *by Him*. The testimony of Christ was confirmed *in them*. It certainly was not being confirmed *by* them, for their actions and conduct were a stench, a contradiction and a reproach upon their testimony for Christ. Paul wants to drive home one salient truth — GRACE. When he takes up the many errors in the church, and pleads with them to judge themselves and repent and forsake their sins, it is only on the basis of the unchangeable grace of an unchangeable God. Because they had been saved by grace, they, therefore, ought to live graciously, not in order to earn salvation or hold on to it or retain it, but because they are saved, sanctified and secure.

And then Paul clinches the entire matter in the next two verses, which we must not miss:

> Who [referring to the Lord Jesus] shall also confirm you unto the end, that ye may be blameless in the day of our Lord Jesus Christ.
> God is faithful, by whom ye were called unto the fellowship of his Son Jesus Christ our Lord (I Corinthians 1:8, 9).

That settles the issue once for all. The Corinthians were far from blameless in their walk and in their conduct. They were carnal, wicked, worldly and contentious; but, says Paul, "God is faithful," in spite of your unfaithfulness. He that hath begun a good work in you will not admit defeat, but will finish it in the end. It will never be said of God that He saved a man, and then couldn't keep him. Ah, no! He will keep on dealing with him and if need be, rebuke that soul, pleading, admonishing, chastening, and even removing by death if necessary, but at the end He *will* present him blameless in the day of Jesus Christ.

We may, then, sum up this introductory passage in I Corinthians by the first three words of verse 9:

## "GOD IS FAITHFUL."

Yes, this is the answer which Paul gives to these immature and worldly Christians: "God is faithful." This is Paul's argument, this is Paul's plea for the Corinthians to repent, to come back from their sinful ways. GOD IS FAITHFUL. Paul is insistent upon this, and says, therefore, that the Lord Jesus "shall confirm you unto the end, that ye may be blameless in the day of our Lord Jesus Christ" (I Corinthians 1:8).

The end result is going to be all that God has purposed it, although it may take chastening and it may take severe dealing on the part of God. Am I speaking to some, who also once knew the joy of the Lord in salvation, but have fallen into ways of sin, and now despair of their own salvation? Do you imagine that you are again lost, and that God has forsaken you? Listen, friend, let me then remind you once again: "God is faithful." He has not forgotten you, but He is waiting even now for you to come as a wandering child, back to the Father's house and home, and His love for you should be the motive for your immediate return.

And so having shown the grace of God, and that He is faithful, even unto the end, Paul concludes with his impassioned plea in verse 10:

> Now I beseech you, brethren, by the name of our Lord Jesus Christ, that ye all speak the same thing, and that there be no divisions among you (I Corinthians 1:10).

Paul could speak in regard to this matter with great boldness, for he himself had been so grateful for the grace of God as exhibited in his life, that he had made the complete and the full surrender so that he could say to these Corinthians:

> Be ye followers of me, even as I also am of Christ (I Corinthians 11:1).

Paul could say, "The love of Christ constraineth us," and this is the motive which should energize our whole lives, and be the driving and impelling urge for our dedication and our service to Him. This is Paul's argument, that because of the "grace of God" which has been so freely bestowed, we should be willing to make the complete surrender (Romans 12:1).

You will notice that it is not a matter of commandment, but a matter of beseeching by the mercies of God. The threatenings of the law and the threatenings of judgment may cause men to refrain from committing sin, but threatenings will never cause them to serve the Lord with obedience and love. This only comes as a result of the appreciation of the greatness of that salvation which the Lord by His wonderful grace has given to us, though we do not merit it and are unworthy of it in every respect.

This is the only cure for carnality and the divisions among Christians today. If we could exercise the love of God as Paul exercised it, and love one another even as God for Christ's sake hath loved us, all of our differences and difficulties would come to an end. It is self-love, instead of love of God; it it self-seeking, instead of seeking the good of others, which is at the root of 90 percent of all of the troubles and difficulties which are vexing God's people, and are so displeasing to our Lord. How long it has taken the Church to learn the lesson that legal restraint and serving the Lord out of a sense of duty will never produce in our hearts the fruits of righteousness. Only that service which is spontaneous and comes as the effortless response of a grateful heart to the goodness of God can be acceptable to Him.

*Chapter Three*

# DID PAUL PRACTICE WATER BAPTISM?

> For Christ sent me not to baptize, but to preach the gospel: not with wisdom of words, lest the cross of Christ should be made of none effect.
>
> For the preaching of the cross is to them that perish foolishness; but unto us which are saved it is the power of God (I Corinthians 1:17, 18).

THERE is always the great danger that in our preaching men will "see" the preacher and the instrument, instead of "hearing the sermon," and the Word of God. There is ever the danger of men's being carried away by the personality of the speaker and missing the message entirely. Paul realized this, and emphasizes the fact that he came not with the wisdom of words, lest their attention be attracted to the instrument and the channel through which God spoke, rather than to the message which God would have them hear. Because of special talent or gift, or because of the attractive personality of the speaker, we may be carried away with admiration and respect for the man, and miss the entire message that God would have us to hear. Too often people leave a service, captivated by the handsomeness of the speaker, or his gracious personality, or his eloquence, and they fail to get the blessing of the message. A story is told of two men who visited London one Lord's day during the days of Charles Haddon Spurgeon. In the morning they visited a London church to hear a renowned gospel preacher. As they left the church one was heard to say, "What a great and wonderful preacher this man is." However, in the evening they went to hear Charles

Haddon Spurgeon, and as they left the tabernacle they were heard to remark, "What a wonderful Christ that man has preached." In the morning they saw a man, and in the evening they saw *the Man,* the Lord Jesus Christ. That is the difference that Paul is seeking to emphasize here.

This was the situation in the church at Corinth, and the occasion for Paul's writing to them. They were carried away by their admiration of individual men, and thus they became carnal in their actions and in their conduct. Paul makes this clear in this chapter. We repeat again the passage for you, as it is the key to the book:

> For it hath been declared unto me of you, my brethren, by them which are of the house of Chloe, that there are contentions among you (I Corinthians 1:11).

And these contentions which resulted in divisions and strife were over men, for Paul continues in verse 12:

> Now this I say, that every one of you saith, I am of Paul; and I of Apollos; and I of Cephas; and I of Christ.
> Is Christ divided? was Paul crucified for you? or were ye baptized in the name of Paul? (I Corinthians 1:12, 13).

There were, therefore, at least four groups in the church at Corinth, contending and striving with one another. One group may be called the "Paulites." They were so taken up with Paul's teaching of grace that they couldn't see anything else, and they imagined that they knew the truth of grace above everyone else. And a second group might be called the "Apollosites." They were undoubtedly captivated and enamored by the eloquence and the pulpit power and oratory of the evangelist, Apollos. They admired his wonderful vocabulary, and his ability to sway the audience from one emotion to another. But they were shallow and saw only the man, and despised those who followed Paul. A third group clung to Peter, and may be called the "Cephasites" or "Peterites." They liked Peter's homely, down-to-earth, impetuous, often crude and legal handling of the Word. But then there was a fourth group who despised all the other three, and said:

"We are of Christ. We do not follow a man, we do not call our group after any individual or system — we are of Christ." Little did they realize that humility and regard for others and tolerance for those who might differ with us is the first mark of Christlikeness, sadly lacking in their own lives, due to spiritual pride, which is the basis for all carnality.

All made one and the same mistake — they saw man instead of Christ. While they each considered themselves better than, and superior to others, Paul says they were acting like little children, and calls them "babies." They were carnal in their conduct. They looked at the flesh instead of at the spirit. And right here we find the seed of sectarianism and denominationalism, both of which are found in the Book of Acts and in the Book of Corinthians. Here are the beginnings of four denominations: Paulites, Apollosites, Cephasites, and Christites. And what a harvest has resulted as evidenced by all the various sects and divisions and separations among Christians today, in the centuries since Pentecost.

## Sectarianism Is Sin

This spirit of sectarianism Paul bemoaned and condemned and sought to stem in the church at Corinth. This he does in a most emphatic way. He says:

> Is Christ divided? was Paul crucified for you? or were ye baptized in the name of Paul? (I Corinthians 1:13).

Is Christ divided? Are not all of these, Paul, Apollos and Peter preaching the same Christ and essentially the same Gospel? Oh, yes, there may be a difference in emphasis, a difference of delivery and treatment or application of the text, but all are one and the same in their purpose. They are laborers together. And so Paul seems to admonish the Corinthian believers by telling them to get their eyes off men, and get together, and fix their eyes only on the perfect Person of the Lord Jesus Christ. And Paul singles out those who admired *him* as the worst offenders. He rebukes his own followers, rather than those who followed Apollos, or Peter, for he says:

> Was Paul crucified for you? or were ye baptized in the name of Paul? (I Corinthians 1:13).

It seems that a great deal of emphasis was placed on water baptism in the Corinthian church. And then, as now, it was a bone of contention. There were some who considered themselves superior to others, because they had been baptized by Paul personally. They either refused to recognize a baptism not performed by the leader of their own group or sect, or felt that they were more holy because they had been baptized by a certain individual. To this Paul replies:

> I thank God that I baptized none of you, but Crispus and Gaius;
>
> Lest any should say that I had baptized in mine own name.
>
> And I baptized also the household of Stephanas: besides, I know not whether I baptized any other.
>
> For Christ sent me not to baptize, but to preach the gospel: not with the wisdom of words, lest the cross of Christ should be made of none effect (I Corinthians 1:14-17).

What tremendous violence has been done to this passage by the "Paulites," who hold up Paul as the one superior apostle above all the other writers of the New Testament. There are even some who would exalt his teaching above the teachings of the Lord Jesus Christ Himself. In trying to get rid of water baptism, they have seized upon this passage to prove their point; but in doing so they have mutilated the Scriptures destroying their own argument. They usually quote:

> I thank God I baptized none of you [PERIOD!]

and cry out, "See here, Paul never baptized anyone at all." But Paul *did* baptize. It seems that all the Corinthians were baptized in water, for Paul says in essence, "In whose name were ye baptized?"

But notice, Paul says that "he" also baptized some of them, and mentions several in particular, Gaius, and Crispus, and the family of Stephanas. Paul *did* baptize, but he was glad that he had not baptized any more of them because they had made it a matter of dispute and argument and contention and division, instead of a matter of unity among the believers. "If you are going to make it an issue, *who* baptized you, then I wish I hadn't baptized any of you," Paul seems to say. And that is the force of the verse by Paul. Water baptism, while preached, taught and practiced by the apostle Paul, was not the main thing for which he was sent. It certainly was not a matter of salvation, and, therefore, certainly not a subject for division, debate and separation from other believers.

## PREACH THE GOSPEL

And then again, it is the common practice of those who would do away with all the ordinances to quote the Scriptures with the wrong interpretation. In verse 17 we read, for instance:

> For Christ sent me not to baptize, but to preach the gospel (I Corinthians 1:17).

Now Paul does not say in this verse that Christ "sent me, telling me *not* to baptize." That is the meaning given to it by the "Paulites." But Paul, while he *did* baptize, had for his prime commission the preaching of the Gospel. Baptism was entirely secondary. Paul believed in it with all his heart, but if they were going to fight about it, he would rather never baptize anyone again, rather than have it made the source of division among believers, "lest the cross of Christ should be made of none effect" (I Corinthians 1:17).

Notice those words carefully: "lest the cross of Christ should be made of none effect." Baptism in its place is a Christian ordinance, but when we pay more attention to baptizing than preaching, it becomes an evil. When we exalt it above the Word of God in all of its fulness, then it becomes a hindrance instead of a help. When we are more interested in making Baptists, or Presbyterians, or Plymouth Brethren, than Christians, we are carnal, fleshly, sectarian and useless.

## WATER BAPTISM

Two things, therefore, are plainly taught in this statement of Paul. The first is that water baptism does have a place in the Christian assembly, and that Paul preached it, and taught it, and practiced it, and expected it of these Corinthian believers. The second great truth, which is often overlooked, is that while it is desirable, it is never to be made the issue for division and strife among believers. Baptism is a testimony of a work which has already been accomplished, and therefore has nothing to do with the obtaining or the retaining of salvation. However, we believe that there is always a joy and a victory in being obedient to the Lord Jesus Christ, and this holds also in the matter of baptism. While we firmly insist that it takes more than water to wash away our sins, and that we are only saved by personal faith in the Lord Jesus Christ, we also believe that it is the desire of our Lord that all such should publicly witness to their identification with our Lord and Saviour in His death and resurrection, and therefore, baptism becomes a testimony of our relationship to the Lord Jesus and not a method of obtaining this relationship. If you feel that baptism should be made a condition for belonging to your local church or assembly, well and good, but *don't* make it a condition for belonging to *the* Church of Jesus Christ, which is His Body. If all concerned would show more grace and tolerance and love toward those who may differ with them in these matters, much of the reproach which is brought upon the Church of Christ today would end.

The sad thing is that so much emphasis has been placed upon ordinances that we have forgotten the plan of salvation, and have exalted these things above the simple message of redemption through faith by grace as the work of God alone. Someone has said that as long as a mule is kicking it makes no progress; and it is certainly true that as long as members of the Body of Christ are quibbling and wrangling and striving among each other, over secondary issues, they can make no progress in the great commission, "Go ye into all the world and preach the gospel to every creature."

## Chapter Four

# THE NATURAL MAN

> But the natural man receiveth not the things of the Spirit
> of God: for they are foolishness unto him: neither can he know
> them, because they are spiritually discerned.
> But he that is spiritual judgeth all things, yet he himself
> is judged of no man.
> For who hath known the mind of the Lord, that he may
> instruct him? But we have the mind of Christ (I Cor. 2:14-16).

THE Bible divides all humanity into two classes, and only
two — saved and lost. The lost man is called the natural
man because he has been born only once of natural parents,
through the line of Adam, man's federal head. The saved
man is called the spiritual man, because he has been born
again from above the second time, by the Spirit of Almighty
God Himself. The natural, unregenerate man possesses the
nature of father Adam. The spiritual man possesses the Spirit
of God, having become a partaker of the divine nature (II
Peter 1:4).

These two natures are forever opposed to one another, and
antagonistic to each other, and they can never blend, they
can never compromise. By our first brith we are depraved,
blind, born in sin, children of wrath, lost, condemned, dead in
trespasses and sins, and helpless as far as saving ourselves is
concerned. However, when we are saved, the Spirit of God
does nothing to this old nature, but instead creates a brand
new nature, the nature of God Himself, sinless, holy, perfect, and places this new nature alongside the old within the
individual. The new nature does not replace the old, it does
not improve the old, but must ultimately overcome and destroy it. Of the old nature with which all of us are born,

**27**

Paul says that we "were by nature the children of wrath, even as others" (Ephesians 2:3).

Concerning this evil, natural heart of man, the Bible plainly states:

> The heart is deceitful above all things, and desperately wicked: who can know it? (Jeremiah 17:9).

And again, the apostle Paul says in his epistle to the Romans, chapter 3, verses 10 to 12:

> There is none righteous, no, not one:
> There is none that understandeth, there is none that seeketh after God.
> They are all gone out of the way, they are together become unprofitable; there is none that doeth good, no, not one.

This is God's own description of the heart of the natural man, born of Adam's fallen race, and dead in trespasses and in sins.

## THE NEW NATURE

So incorrigibly corrupt is this old nature by our first birth, that even God Himself does not attempt to improve it, fix it up, repair or reform it. He ignores the old nature as being absolutely hopeless and incorrigible, and so instead of seeking to improve it, he creates a brand new thing, called the "new creation." It is a brand new nature, wholly distinct from the old Adamic nature, and God places this new nature of the new man within and alongside the old. Paul says in II Corinthians 5:17:

> Therefore if any man be in Christ, he is a new creature: old things are passed away; behold, all things are become new.

The word "creature" in this verse should be rendered "creation," so that the verse should read: "Therefore if any man be in Christ, he is a new *creation*."

The new man, the regenerate man, lives in a spiritual realm, infinitely above and distinct from the natural. His eyes are opened to spiritual things, his ears to spiritual truths. He sees things to which the natural eye is totally blind, and the

natural ear is totally deaf. This is the force of Paul's statement in verses 9, 10:

> Eye [the natural eye] hath not seen, nor ear [the natural ear]
> heard, neither hath entered into the heart of man, the things
> which God hath prepared for them that love him.
> BUT GOD HATH REVEALED THEM UNTO US BY HIS SPIRIT.

Regeneration, therefore, is a supernatural act of God whereby a spiritual creation takes place, and we behold things which
are utterly unknown and must remain completely unknown
even to the most cultured, sophisticated, educated of those of
Adam's race who have never experienced the new birth.

And now we come to see the striking contrast in our Scripture. The natural man, the unregenerated man, sees none
of these glories of this Book and of salvation and of God's
plan of redemption. He lives in an entirely different world,
the world of sense and of sight, touch and sound. The tangible world is the habitat of the natural man in his unregenerate state, and he is, therefore, totally ignorant of the spiritual
realm which transcends all of these things. And so our Scripture plainly says:

> But the natural man receiveth not the things of the Spirit
> of God: for they are foolishness unto him: neither can he
> know them, because they are spiritually discerned (I Cor. 2:14).

Notice carefully the closing words of this verse: *"They are
spiritually discerned."* Until, therefore, a man has been born
from above, born of the water and the Spirit, he remains
totally blind to spiritual truth. Jesus Himself said to one of
the most cultured, educated, religious leaders of His day:

> Except a man be born again, he cannot SEE (John 3:3).

## NOT HUMAN WISDOM

And right here is the answer to the question, Why are so
many wise, cultured, educated men and women unable to
see the great spiritual truths of the Word of God — the infallible inspiration of the Bible, the virgin birth, the aton-
ing death, the bodily resurrection, the second coming of
Christ, and many other related truths? These things are

utter foolishness to many of the intelligentsia, even to scholars and students of the Bible, while they are patent and clear to the simplest believer in the Lord Jesus. It is all because "spiritual" things can only be seen by spiritual eyes, which have been illumined by the Spirit of God. The natural man, thus, cannot know the things of the Spirit.

There are hundreds and hundreds of sincere persons, honest in their doubts, who are educated and wizards in the knowledge of natural things, in the arts and sciences, who see absolutely nothing supernatural in the Word of God, and see nothing of the great truths of redemption by the blood of the Lord Jesus Christ. All of these things are foolishness to the wise of this world. There are many scholars who are near geniuses in the realm of natural knowledge, who are totally ignorant of God's will as revealed in the Word of God. They may even know the Bible by heart, be able to read it in Hebrew or Greek, admire it for its literary beauty, extol it for its moral and ethical teaching, acknowledge it for its historical and geographical accuracy and precision, and yet not get one inkling or glimpse of the real message of the Book — redemption by faith in the shed blood of the Lord Jesus Christ, the Substitute for sinners. To them the plan of salvation is only foolishness, and the Cross becomes an offense because it humiliates and debases human nature to the place where it belongs. It is possible to admire the person of the Lord Jesus, to preach Him as the flower of humanity, admire His perfect life, and to extol all of His virtues and teach that He died for a principle, and was a martyr to a noble cause, and still miss the spiritual message and the real purpose of the Book, that "Christ Jesus came into the world to save sinners" (I Timothy 1:15).

To know spiritual things, one must be spiritually revived, re-created, and born again. Without the new birth, man never rises above the physical and the psychic. Here is right where modern psychology and psychiatry break down completely. They recognize only the physical and the psychic, and explain all of man's troubles as either physical or psychic, bodily or mental. But there is another realm, a superior realm, a third plane, a higher plane, the spiritual plane which is completely ignored, yet this spiritual plane is just as real, and even more so, than the physical and psychical, and transcends it so far that only the spiritual man is able to apprehend it. This realm is entered through a new birth, by personal faith in the Word of the living God concerning the Lord Jesus.

## THE BIBLE A CLOSED BOOK

I trust that I have awakened some of you to your need of the new birth. You are willing to admit you cannot make head or tail of the Bible or the plan of salvation, and you read it with little profit, and turn from it in disgust. You read the Bible but it means nothing to you at all. It is only a literary exercise, and nothing beyond this is accomplished. You cannot understand it. You tell me, "It's all Greek to me. It does not make sense." Then listen. You need your spiritual eyes opened, for the Bible is for the spiritual people. You need to be born again, and you can be. Now listen carefully. First, you must accept by faith what the Bible says about you. You must bow before the verdict of the Word of God, without any questionings and any doubts. Faith is the death blow to our own natural reason. Faith in the Word of God and in the Lord Jesus Christ, by which we can be saved, means a negation of our own logic and our own philosophy. We must in simple faith believe that the Word of God is the Word of God. This is the very reason that so many refuse to accept the Word, because it is a humbling experience to be born from above. It means that man must admit he is so hopelessly and helplessly lost that there is nothing he can do, no matter how high he may have climbed up the ladder of wisdom and human education and culture, that can save him, until he becomes dead to self and receives by faith that which the Lord Himself has revealed in the Book.

When God creates anything, He always begins with nothing. God will not use any pre-existent material, but God's creations are all "new" creations. When He created the earth in the beginning, and the heavens, He created them out of nothing, and even hung the world upon nothing. So, too, it is with the new creation. If God is to save you, you must become nothing first. Hannah said in her prayer of thanksgiving in I Samuel 2:

> The Lord killeth, and maketh alive: he bringeth down to the grave, and bringeth up.
> The Lord maketh poor, and maketh rich: he bringeth low, and lifteth up (I Samuel 2:6, 7).

Before God can make alive, He must first put to death all of self, and all reliance upon self. I repeat, when God creates a new thing, he always begins with nothing. Until a sinner abandons all hope of his own ability to save himself, the Lord himself cannot do anything for him. So the first step in salvation is to abandon all hope of being saved by one's own works or effort or merit or culture or education or virtue or any other human righteousness, and to cast one's self completely and totally in utter helplessness upon the mercy and the love and the grace of God provided for man through the Cross of Calvary and His resurrection. All of this may be yours upon condition of personal faith. Will you believe right now that Jesus Christ died for you, in your place, and paid for your sins, and rose again? Will you accept this finished work and believe His Word which says:

> Verily, verily, I say unto you, He that heareth my word, and believeth on him that sent me, hath everlasting life, and shall not come into condemnation; but is passed from death unto life (John 5:24).

Just so long as man's pride keeps him from admitting his utter hopelessness and helplessness, just so long he cannot be saved. Only as we come in absolute faith to Him, and abandon all hope of our own salvation, can we be saved.

*Chapter Five*

# DIVINE MATHEMATICS

And I, brethren, could not speak unto you as unto spiritual, but as unto carnal, even as unto babes in Christ.

I have fed you with milk, and not with meat: for hitherto ye were not able to bear it, neither yet now are ye able (I Corinthians 3:1, 2).

THERE are only two kinds of people in the world, saved and lost, born once and born twice, those on the way to heaven and those on the way to hell. The lost are called "natural men" because they have had only a natural birth. The saved are called "spiritual men" because they have in addition to the first birth had a second, spiritual, new birth from above. The born-again man, however, still retains his old nature, called also "the old man," and the "flesh," as well as the new nature, or the divine nature, which came from above. This fact of the two natures is the reason for two kinds of believers — carnal and spiritual. A carnal believer is a saved man who is still controlled, in a measure at least, by the old nature within him, and he gives heed to the old, Adamic nature rather than submitting himself to the new, spiritual nature. The spiritual believer, however, is one who has gained the victory over the old nature, and has enthroned the spiritual, and claimed victory over the flesh, and is walking in the newness of life. The carnal believer is *in* the light, but is not "walking *in*" the light, while the spiritual believer in addition to being *in* the light positionally, is also walking and making progress in the light.

## CARNALITY DEFINED

The church of God in Corinth was a carnal church. Its members walked after the flesh instead of after the spirit.

33

They were saved, but they were still carnal and fleshly, and walked as babes. Paul calls them "the church of God," "sanctified," and "saints" (I Corinthians 1:2). In our Scripture, I Corinthians 3:1, he calls them "brethren." We must, therefore, remember that whatever rebuke these Corinthians needed, they were still the children of God.

The word "carnality" comes from the Greek word "sarx", meaning "flesh." In the setting of our passage, it is synonomous with the old Adamic nature with which we were born of the flesh the first time. When believers give way to this old nature which is still in them, even after the new birth, instead of walking in the Spirit and in the light of God's Word, they become carnal in their conduct and condition. Now carnality expresses itself in two opposite ways. Sometimes it manifests itself in worldliness and indulgence of the sins of the flesh. Most people naturally think carnality expresses itself primarily in this way, and they speak of the worldly believer who lives in sin and indulges in questionable practices as a "carnal" Christian.

However, Paul's idea of a carnal believer in I Corinthians 3 is quite the opposite from this common notion. Carnality in Corinth manifested itself not so much in worldliness and sinful practices as in a "holier than thou" attitude toward others which the Corinthians held in their spiritual pride and boasting. They were proud of the fact that they did *not* indulge in worldly practices. They prided themselves that they were superior to others, and they became separatistic, contentious and proud in their conduct. The Corinthians were divided, therefore, into sects and groups and cliques, each despising the other, resulting in divisions among them.

Paul's answer to this tragic state of affairs was pointed and direct, for he says:

> Who then is Paul, and who is Apollos, but ministers [servants] by whom ye believed, even as the Lord gave to every man?
> I have planted, Apollos watered; but God gave the increase (I Corinthians 3:5, 6).

Who, then, is Paul? Who, then, is Apollos? that you should follow after a man, and not after Christ? They are only channels and instruments whom God chose to accomplish His purpose. God uses different instrumentalities, different men, different talents, different approaches, different personalities, but everything still depends upon the blessing of the Spirit of God. And so Paul's admonition seems to be, Get your eyes off the instrument, and place them alone on the Lord Jesus Christ. He accuses these Corinthians of acting like little children. He tells them that they are silly in their childish admiration of human personalities, and that they have entirely overlooked and missed the message with which these men have been intrusted by the Spirit of God.

### HIGHER MATHEMATICS

Now listen to Paul's amazing argument in the following verses:

> I have planted, Apollos watered; but God gave the increase.
> So then neither is he that planteth any thing [he is a "zero"], neither he that watereth [another "zero"]; but God that giveth the increase (I Corinthians 3:6, 7).

Paul says that he is absolutely nothing by himself. He is nothing but a "zero." He also asserts that Apollos is nothing by himself — he also is a "zero." They are both "zero," nothing, nil. Apart from God and the Spirit of God, all of their talents, all of their abilities, Paul's logic and Apollos' oratory, are only empty words and phrases. Remember, Paul is a "zero" and Apollos a "zero." That is the meaning of:

> So then neither is he that planteth any thing [zero], neither he that watereth [zero].

Both are nothing, and together they are still nothing, for zero plus zero still equals zero.

But now notice an example of divine calculation and mathematics. Here is the answer which Paul gives in a striking manner.

> Now he that planteth and he that watereth are ONE (I Corinthians 3:8).

Here Paul says that zero and zero equal *one*. Two zeros can be something, if they are placed in relation to the digit *one*. We have already shown that Paul is a zero, and Apollos is a zero, and yet Paul and Apollos together, when in the proper relation to Christ, become something. Now Christ, of course, is the ONE, the only ONE. Without Him Paul and Apollos and Cephas are absolutely nothing; by themselves and collectively they still amount to only one big zero. But now add the digit ONE, the Lord Jesus Christ, and the zeros immediately become something. That one digit makes the difference. If we take a zero and place after it the numeral one, we have .01, or one one-hundredth. It isn't much, but it is after all something. Now take two zeros, and add the numeral one, and we have .001, or one one-thousandth. The more zeros we place before the one, the less the amount. The more of Paul and Apollos we place before Christ, the only One, the less Christ amounts to, and the less we shall see of Him.

But now let us reverse these figures. Instead of putting the zeros before the one (Christ), let us place the one before the zero, and then we have 10 — ten. Nothing has now become ten. There has been a tenfold increase in value. If we add two zeros after the one (add Paul and Apollos after Christ) then we have one hundred — we increase again tenfold. The more zeros we place BEHIND the one, the greater the increase — tenfold each time. You see it all depends upon WHERE we put the Lord Jesus Christ. If the minister comes first, Christ diminishes. If Christ is first, we lose sight of the servant, his virtues as well as his shortcomings, and we see only Christ.

And now one other thing. If we add one zero to the one, we have ten, but the more zeros we add, the greater Christ becomes, and so Paul concludes this section with the remarkable words:

For we are labourers *together* with God: ye are God's husbandry, ye are God's building.

According to the grace of God which is given unto me, as a wise masterbuilder, I have laid the foundation, and another buildeth thereon. But let every man take heed how he buildeth thereupon (I Corinthians 3:9, 10).

## LABORERS TOGETHER

We are laborers *together*. God uses Paul and Apollos and Peter, and all the other instruments and gifts to the Church. They have different personalities, they have different appeals, they have different abilities, but all are preaching the one and the same Christ. And after all, it is the message which counts, and not the messenger. As we become occupied with Him, we begin to lose sight of the instrument entirely. And this is the cure for all sectarianism and the evils of denominationalism. We must become so occupied with Christ and His program, so busy preaching HIM, and recommending HIM to sinners, that we have no time to quibble over minor issues and hair-splitting differences, or to bicker over non-essential doctrines, and engage in profitless arguments. We then can differ on many, many issues, and disagree on many minor points, but we can still be so united in the one great program of the Gospel and the exaltation of the person of the Lord Jesus that we count these things as nothing. Holding Him aloft, we are submerged completely until men see not us, but only the Christ.

This is the desperate need of the Church today. We are so busy defending our sectarian dogmas, so busy promoting our own doctrinal positions, so busy building our sect or denomination or group, that we have left off presenting the Lord Jesus Christ. We are more zealous in making church members than in getting people saved from the awfulness of sin and eternal condemnation.

Oh, for the spirit of a Paul, oh, for a revival of charity and love and tolerance for other true believers who may differ with us on points which are not essential or basic in the matter of salvation. Oh, for the spirit of a John who said:

He must increase, but I must decrease (John 3:30).

God grant that we may realize that we "are labourers together with God: we are God's husbandry, we are God's building."

We have but to observe the example of the Lord Jesus Christ and realize the group with which He chose to carry out His ministry while here on earth. He chose twelve apostles, in addition to His seventy disciples. When we consider their differences in personality and in temperament, we can learn a great lesson of unity of cooperation in spite of diversity of personality. What a difference there was between John and Peter, yet the Lord was willing to use both of them, and He carried out His program through these two utterly different and divergent personalities. We must remember that God has not cast us all into the same mold, and God has a place for all of us in carrying out His plan of salvation. The great tragedy in our lives is that we try to pattern everyone after our own selves, and, therefore, in our struggle for uniformity we forget the diversity which God uses in accomplishing His divine purpose. Truly the Lord Jesus said:

That they all may be one; as thou, Father, art in me, and I in thee, that they also may be one in us . . .

. . . that they may be one, even as we are one (John 17: 21, 22).

And this does not mean giving up personality, for God uses one for this, and one for that, one to plant, one to water, one to harvest, one to sow, and another to reap. May God grant us grace that we may know our own particular, peculiar place in the program of God, and do it.

## Chapter Six

# GOLD, SILVER AND PRECIOUS STONES

> For other foundation can no man lay than that is laid, which is Jesus Christ.
>
> Now if any man build upon this foundation gold, silver, precious stones, wood, hay, stubble;
>
> Every man's work shall be made manifest: for the day shall declare it, because it shall be revealed by fire; and the fire shall try every man's work of what sort it is.
>
> If any man's work abide which he hath built thereupon, he shall receive a reward.
>
> If any man's work shall be burned, he shall suffer loss: but he himself shall be saved; yet so as by fire (I Corinthians 3:11-15).

THE apostle Paul is speaking in this passage only about born-again believers, those who have experienced the new birth, and does not have in mind at all those who are still unsaved. The Corinthians were a carnal lot, but they were believers nevertheless. They were split up into sects and cliques and different groups, but Paul appeals to them on the basis of the fact that they are believers on the Lord Jesus, to stop these childish practices of following men and exaggerating their differences. He says, "All of us, myself, Apollos, Peter, are doing the same job, albeit in a different way. But we are laborers together nevertheless. We all preach the same Christ, and you who have believed, whether through the teaching of Paul, or the preaching of Apollos or by the exhortations of Peter, are all resting on the same foundation. Why then are you divided and contentious and bickering and arguing and splitting hairs." Paul says:

> For other foundation can no man lay than that is laid, which is Jesus Christ (I Corinthians 3:11).

He reminds them that they are saved, resting on the Rock, Christ Jesus. This however, gives them no license to live as they please. Their being saved by grace is no excuse for carnality and careless living, and living a life of worldliness and pride. The fact that they are secure by the grace of God does not justify sectarianism or spiritual pride by any means. And to clinch this, Paul reminds them of the coming judgment of believers. Now, of course, this truth may shock some of our ultra-grace scholars, but there is a future judgment for all believers. While the believer will never be judged as to his salvation by faith in the Lord Jesus, which is forever settled, and will never appear at the judgment of the Great White Throne, he will nevertheless be called into account for his conduct *after* he has been saved. He will render an account of what he has done *with* his salvation. He will have to be judged on the basis of his faithfulness in using his talents and his time and possessions for the Lord. This judgment is called the "Judgment Seat of Christ." We have it mentioned in II Corinthians 5:10,

> For we must all appear before the judgment seat of Christ; that every one may receive the things done in the body, according to that he hath done, whether it be good or bad.

This judgment will take place following the coming of the Lord for His Church in the air. It will concern rewards or loss of rewards. It will have nothing to do whatsoever with salvation or our eternal destiny. That was forever settled at the Cross, and appropriated by the grace of God. This judgment will determine our position in the kingdom at the reign of Christ, and the rewards which we will receive at His hand. The Judgment Seat of Christ, therefore, answers the question which so many people are asking, What about Christians who are saved, and then live carnal worldly lives, and fall into sin? Are they still saved, or do they lose their salvation? What will happen to them? The answer is the Judgment Seat of

Christ. It forever silences the accusation that the preaching of grace makes for careless living. Ah, no! There is a reckoning coming for believers and for some it will not be pleasant.

## ON BASIS OF WORKS

And so Paul says concerning all who have taken Christ as their Saviour and their Lord, and are resting on the eternal foundation Rock:

> Let every man take heed how he buildeth thereupon (I Corinthians 3:10b).

Here then is a solemn warning to believers to *take heed*. Don't you believe it, says Paul, when the Devil whispers that because you are saved by grace, you can be careless or indifferent or live as you please.

There are two general classes of believers who will appear at this Judgment Seat of Christ: those who will receive a reward for faithfulness, and others who will "suffer loss" and see their works destroyed by fire. Paul uses a strikingly contrasting figure to describe these two classes. He first mentions those who build on this foundation, "gold, silver and precious stones." Next he mentions those who build on this same foundation, "hay, wood and stubble." The contrast is indeed amazing and striking. We are to remember that both of them are building on the one foundation, and therefore, are safe as far as eternity is concerned. But the super-structure, that which they build upon the foundation, will be subjected to the testing fires of the Judgment Seat of Christ.

There are many facets of truth contained in this contrast, but we have space to mention only a few of them. Notice first of all that the first group (gold, silver and precious stones) consists of products of a creative act. These were placed here by God in creation. They are not the result of growth, but creation. They are not the result of development, but were placed here as such in the beginning. They represent the things of the Spirit, and of the new creation, and of the new life in Christ Jesus. They represent the fruits of the new birth, and are, therefore, permanent in their nature.

But notice that the products of the second group (hay, wood and stubble) are the result of natural growth and development. They were not created in the form in which they appear, but are the result of a process of natural growth. They are the things of the old nature, and of the natural man. They are the things which come out of the earth by development and growth, and which belong to the flesh, and to the carnal fleshly man. Paul describes these as the works of the flesh (Galatians 5:19). In Corinth they are "contentions, envyings, strife, bickerings and criticism." But the gold, silver and precious stones are the fruits of the new life in Christ.

Then notice a very striking second contrast. The gold, silver and precious stones are costly, but they are not bulky or massive. Only a little of them has a great value. I can carry a million dollars worth of precious stones in my pocket and you would never suspect or know that I have it on my person. Precious Stones have great value, but they do not loom large in the eyes of men. Now notice the difference in the second group, of "hay, wood and stubble." They are big and bulky and massive, imposing, but relatively worthless. A barn full of stubble would not be worth the price of moving it. A whole load of hay or wood is worth less than the smallest diamond. The second group represents the works of the flesh which men measure in terms of bigness and imposing massiveness. I can hide a fortune in precious stones, so you cannot see them, while a stack of hay can be seen a mile away. But God says the precious stones alone will abide. How prone we are to appraise things in terms of bigness and mass and in the bulk, and overlook the little precious things which go unobserved. We see the crowds, we see the numbers, we count the converts, but God sees the gold of that precious shut-in, isolated from the world, almost forgotten, who carries on the all-important ministry of prayer, and intercession, which is the secret of the massive results.

There is a day of reckoning coming when our motives shall be judged, when our accomplishments shall be weighed in the light of, not what we have accomplished but what we *might* have accomplished. The servant with one talent who gained only one more will be rewarded, while the one with ten talents who used only five of them will suffer loss. God is not interested in quantity as much as He is interested in quality. A little gold, inconspicuous but precious, is worth far more than a warehouse full of hay and stubble. It is faithfulness which will be rewarded, the fruit which remains.

### PERISHABLE THINGS

Which brings us in conclusion to one other distinction between these two classes at the Judgment Seat of Christ. The "gold, silver and precious stones" are permanent, and will abide. The "hay, wood and stubble" will all have to perish and go up in smoke. Only that which is done in the Spirit shall stand the test of the Judgment Seat of the Lord Jesus Christ. That which has been done in the energy of the flesh, no matter how flashy or impressive it may have been, no matter how men have acclaimed it, the Lord who judges the heart will appraise everything on the basis of the motive and the faithfulness with which it has been accomplished. The humble believer who serves God in his own little corner, in the kitchen, around the farm, or in the office, because of his love for God, without thought of human plaudits or appreciation, shall shine in glory there, even more than those who have been endowed with much greater talents, and yet have not used them to the full for the service of God. And be not deceived, that which is done for the sake of personal gain or popularity or influence, or its impression upon men, will go up in smoke, for only that which is done for Christ will last. Jesus said:

> Ye have not chosen me, but I have chosen you, and ordained you, that ye should go and bring forth fruit, and that *your fruit should remain* (John 15:16).

The final test of our service will be the fruit which remains at the Judgment Seat of Christ. There was a time in my early ministry when I frequently made the remark, "There is no greater joy that can come to a servant of God than to lead a soul to Christ." As the years passed by, and we observed some of the apparent results of our ministry, we have changed our estimate of the greatest joy which can come to anyone in the service of the Lord. There is a greater joy than leading a soul to Christ, and that is, to come back ten, fifteen, twenty, twenty-five, and thirty years later, and to find those same precious souls going on for Christ. John said:

> I have no greater joy than to hear that my children walk in truth (III John 4).

It is, therefore, the fruit which remains which will only show up at the Judgment Seat of Christ, and the rest which has been only due to other motives will be utterly lacking. John says that it is a joy to "hear that his children are walking in the truth." There is a great deal of difference between standing in the truth and walking in the truth. We hear a great deal these days about our standing in Christ, and our security in Christ, and we rejoice and revel in our position; and yet it is possible just to stand without walking and making progress in Him. We shall have to be judged on the basis of the abiding fruit. All believers who have trusted in the finished work of the Lord Jesus are safe in their standing, but all are not progressive in their walking. May the Lord grant us to keep our eyes upon the reward as well as upon the loss of reward, and remember that, "it is required in stewards, that a man be found faithful" (I Corinthians 4:2).

## Chapter Seven

# HAY, WOOD AND STUBBLE

> For we must all appear before the judgment seat of Christ; that every one may receive the things done in his body, according to that he hath done, whether it be good or bad (II Corinthians 5:10).

THERE is a day of reckoning coming for believers when every child of God shall give an account of his walk, his life, his conduct, and his accomplishments, after he was saved. It will not involve salvation, but only rewards or the loss of rewards. In our previous study we saw that:

> Every man's work shall be made manifest: for the day shall declare it, because it shall be revealed by fire; and the fire shall try every man's work of what sort it is (I Corinthians 3:13).

The service we have rendered out of love for Christ and our fellowmen will be rewarded, while the service which has been performed for personal honor or applause or gain or self-gratification will all be destroyed in the fires of the Judgment Seat of Christ.

As believers we are all builders upon the one foundation, Jesus Christ, and being on that foundation we are forever safe, for the foundation is indestructible, having been laid from all eternity. But that which we build upon this foundation must pass the test of God's judgment and estimate. We hear a great deal about the "rewards" of the believer at the Judgment Seat of Christ, but we hear very little about those who shall "suffer loss." This is not as popular a subject, and therefore, it is oftentimes neglected and overlooked and passed by.

45

Countless sermons have been preached on the five crowns for believers, but there is a dearth of teaching among Christians on what will happen to those who do not receive these crowns. As a result many believers are careless and indifferent, believing that it will make no difference in the end. If they are faithful, they reason, they will be rewarded, but if they fail, well, they are still saved, and will go to heaven in the end, and everything will be forgotten. But the Bible teaches no such strange doctrine. Instead, Paul says very definitely:

> If any man's work shall be burned, he shall suffer loss: but he himself shall be saved; yet so as by fire (I Corinthians 3:15).

I confess I do not know all that is implied in this verse by the expressions, "man's work shall be burned," and "suffer loss," and "saved . . . so as by fire." But even though we may not know fully what these figures actually represent, one thing is crystal clear — it will be a terrible calamity for believers to suffer loss when they might have had something that would abide at the Judgment Seat of Christ. It certainly will not be a pleasant experience to "suffer" loss. It does not say "enjoy" loss, but says *suffer* loss. What regrets are implied in this prospect! After a lifetime of opportunity, to meet the Saviour empty-handed, and to be ashamed at His appearing! After years of being saved, to meet Christ and not to have confidence to meet Him! To be saved like Lot by the skin of the teeth!

Oh, believer, consider this. One of these days the Lord Jesus will come, and you will have to give an account of the opportunities you have had, what you have done with your talents, your time, and yes, your material possessions. Have you given your talents to Him, or have you used them only for self, and your God-given abilities just for personal gain and gratification? Have you given of your time in prayer and testimony, and in witnessing, or has it been only to gratify the flesh in seeking the pleasures of this life, and the comforts of the flesh? Have you used your ability to make money (a God-given talent) to further the Gospel, recognizing that all you have is from Him, or have you spent it in your search for pleasure, comforts, luxuries, or even the fleshly gratification of just seeing your possessions multiply? Remember, the Bible says we shall give an account:

> For we *must* all appear before the judgment seat of Christ; that every one may receive the things done in his body, according to that he hath done, whether it be good or bad (II Corinthians 5:10).

I repeat that we may not know all that is involved by the expression, "but he himself shall be saved; yet so as by fire." I do not know whether this is a figure of some terrible ordeal through which we will have to pass, of remorse and self-accusation, or some other form of chastening. We do not know; but the text implies that the experience will be an unpleasant one.

We must also repeat that the Judgment Seat of Christ is not a matter of salvation. God does not force any of His followers to be faithful by threats of punishment or the loss of salvation. He wants our service to be voluntary, and out of a heart of love and gratitude, and not under threat or duress.

## TEMPLES OF GOD

And yet, even though the motive for service must be love and devotion and gratitude for the grace of God bestowed upon us, Paul feels constrained to add a grave and a serious warning. He wants us to know the consequences if we "neglect so great salvation." He would have us —

> . . . work out your own salvation with fear and trembling.
> For it is God which worketh in you both to will and to do of his good pleasure (Philippians 2:12, 13).

We are not to work *for* our salvation, but we are to work it *out*. Salvation is God's gift, it is free, and what we do with it is our responsibility. And to emphasize this fact, that we belong to God and are responsible, Paul adds:

> Know ye not that ye are the temple of God, and that the Spirit of God dwelleth in you? (I Corinthians 3:16).

Paul's plea to believers to live holy, consecrated, dedicated lives is made upon the fact that they are the possession of God. They are God's temple, the dwelling place of the Almighty. I wonder if we have not missed the impact of this great truth. This body in which we live here below is God's temple. God lives in you, and God lives in me. God's Spirit has chosen to make my body His home. How then can we use this body for selfish, sinful desires? To take God's house, and to use it for anything but God's glory is a contradiction. And so he warns us in the next verse:

> If any man defile the temple of God, him shall God destroy; for the temple of God is holy, which temple ye are (I Corinthians 3:17).

Now this verse has been the occasion for much misunderstanding among believers. Some infer from this that for one to defile the body by sin means that God will cause such an one to be lost again. This is the interpretation given to the word "destroy" as used in this verse. On the surface this might seem to be true, but we must take the verse in the light of the context in which Paul is speaking. We must ask, What is Paul talking about? In the previous verse Paul tells us that all the works of the flesh will be destroyed, burned up at the Judgment Seat of Christ, but the believer "himself shall be saved." Now the Lord cannot go back on that word, when He says that even though all the works may be destroyed, nevertheless the believer "himself shall be saved." That is a positive fact. Paul is still talking about this in verse 17. He tells us that it is possible for a believer to so defile the body, the temple of God, that rather than let him continue in his sin, God will destroy "the body." God may take such an one by death, prematurely, as a part of His chastening. It is not a destruction of the individual but a destruction of the body which has been defiled. This is clearly taught also in I Corinthians 5. In dealing with a believer who lived in open sin, Paul instructs the church "to deliver such an one unto Satan for the destruction of the flesh, that the spirit may be saved in the day of the Lord Jesus" (I Corinthians 5:5).

## ETERNALLY SAVED

The verses of this chapter which follow, therefore, emphasize this great truth of God's dealing with carnal believers, in not casting them away, but in "chastening" them, as Paul states in I Corinthians 11:32!

> But when we are judged, we are chastened of the Lord, that we should not be condemned with the world (I Corinthians 11:32).

God loves His children too much to permit them to continue in carnality and sin. Rather than allow them to go on in defilement, He may take His child home by the way of death to answer for his conduct at the Judgment Seat of Christ. And so Paul concludes:

> Let no man deceive himself. If any man among you seemeth to be wise in this world, let him become a fool, that he may be wise.
>
> For the wisdom of this world is foolishness with God. For it is written, He taketh the wise in their own craftiness.
>
> And again, The Lord knoweth the thoughts of the wise, that they are vain.
>
> Therefore let no man glory in men. For all things are yours;
>
> Whether Paul, or Apollos, or Cephas, or the world, or life, or death, or things present, or things to come; all are yours;
>
> And ye are Christ's; and Christ is God's (I Corinthians 3: 18-23).

Surely the argument of Paul here is unmistakable, that in spite of God's dealing and chastening with His children, and while He demands righteousness in walk and in conduct, He will not go back on His grace, by which we are saved. And, therefore, He seems to say, "Oh, you Corinthians, because you belong to Christ, why not cease from your carnality and repent from your sins, and turn from your wicked ways, lest your stubbornness necessitate the chastening of the Lord, and you suffer loss in that day when Jesus comes." In the light of this truth, therefore, they were to search their own hearts, and set their house in order, lest the Lord come upon them with a rod.

We realize that this neglected truth is one which is not welcome among believers. We love to hear about the security we have in Christ, and all the graces which He has bestowed upon us, and all the privileges which are ours as members of the family of God. But too often we are loathe to assume the responsibilities which all of this sonship implies. There is no question that if the average believer in the average church could be more conscious of the fact that every act and every moment, and every talent which he possesses is to pass before the Judgment Seat of Christ, an end would be made to much of the worldliness and sinfulness, and carelessness on the part of believers. We need to recognize the fact that God would have His people clean, and if they are not willing to cleanse themselves by the washing of the water by the Word, the Lord will have to use other means.

Therefore, it is the duty of every believer to search his own heart for every single known and doubtful sin in his life, and then to apply the promises of God and the washing of the water by the Word, come clean before Him, and not be ashamed before Him at His coming. John tells us in I John 1:9;

> If we confess our sins, he is faithful and just to forgive us our sins, and to cleanse us from all unrighteousness (I John 1:9).

This is the easy way of coming to Him, and availing ourselves of the cleansing power of the Spirit of God through the Word of God, on the basis of the shed blood of the Lord Jesus Christ. John tells us that,

> If we walk in the light, as he is in the light, we have fellowship one with another, and the blood of Jesus Christ his Son cleanseth us from all sin (I John 1:7).

Again we would like to emphasize the expression, "walk in the light." Too often people are just satisfied with being in the Light. Too many Christians have a mean and low and base idea of salvation, as though it were merely escaping the judgment fires of hell. They do not seem to have any vision of service and fruit-bearing in this life. They are content to be in the light, and to stand in the light, but not to "walk" in the light. And so John tells us very definitely under inspiration,

> If we *walk in the light* . . . we have fellowship one with another, and the blood of Jesus Christ his Son cleanseth us from all sin (I John 1:7).

May the Lord help us never to be satisfied until we can see progress in our life day by day. As you look back over your spiritual life, and your experience since the day of your conversion, can you see any progress, or is there only retrogression or standing still? Do you love the Lord as much as you did those first few weeks after your salvation experience and your meeting with Him? Is the Bible as precious now as then? Do you spend as much time in prayer? Is there as much love for the Lord as expressed in love for the brethren, as in those times? It is well that we take stock of ourselves, and see whether we are making progress; for, after all, there is no standing still in the Christian life.

*Chapter Eight*

# THE GRACE OF GOD

For who maketh thee to differ from another? and what hast thou that thou didst not receive? now if thou didst receive it, why dost thou glory, as if thou hadst not received it (I Corinthians 4:7).

THE Corinthian church was a carnal church, and given to the works of the flesh. The members were puffed up and prided themselves in the abundance of gifts of the Spirit bestowed upon them. They were puffed up because they spoke in tongues, because among them were many with the gift of healing and miracles and prophecies and interpretation of tongues. But instead of becoming humble in the knowledge of God's wonderful grace bestowed upon them, they exalted themselves and despised others who did not possess the same gifts which they themselves enjoyed. They sat in judgment upon other believers, because they did not possess the same manifestations. And thus they spoiled everything, and the result was division, envying, strife, criticism, and condemnation of one another.

For this reason, Paul writes to them and calls them "babes in Christ." Instead of being what they prided themselves to be, mature, strong Christians, superior to others, Paul says, With all your gifts and manifestations, you are just spiritual cry-babies, unable to appreciate the grace of God to its fullness. For this reason, I have fed you with milk, and not with meat.

## THE GRACE OF GOD

The remedy for this condition is an understanding of the true meaning of the grace of God. When we understand

God's grace, and that everything we are is by the grace of God, fault-finding, criticism, gossip and judging of one another comes to an end. Paul, therefore, pleads with them not to pass judgment upon any brother until the Lord comes and sets up the Judgment Seat of Christ. Until then, we are totally incompetent to judge fairly on any matter whatsoever. We remind you again that this spirit of criticism and condemnation was the result of carnality, the mistake of following men instead of the Head, which is Christ. Some exalted Paul to the skies, and despised Apollos. Others were enamored with the eloquence of Apollos but despised Paul. The remedy, however, is Christ — and to cease from judging anything now, but to labor together in harmony.

## FIRST APPLICATION

The effectiveness of Paul's plea and argument lay in the fact that Paul practiced what he preached. Paul was the last one to judge his fellow believers. He sought rather to examine his own heart, and to be clean and perfect before God. And so we can understand his words:

> And these things [not to judge others], brethren, I have in a figure transferred to myself and to Apollos for your sakes; that ye might learn in us not to think of men above that which is written, that no one of you be puffed up for one against another (I Corinthians 4:6).

Paul applies this warning against judging others and taking sides to the situation in the church at Corinth. There were those who favored Paul, others who favored Apollos, and the bitterness of feeling threatened to split the church. Now, says Paul, apply my advice in this situation, that "no one of you be puffed up for one against another."

Notice the words, "for one against another." The followers of Paul were puffed up against the adherents of Apollos, and vice versa. And then Paul comes to the heart of the entire matter in verse 7, and says:

> For who maketh thee to differ from another? and what hast thou that thou didst not receive? now if thou didst receive it,

why dost thou glory, as if thou hadst not received it (I Corinthians 4:7).

## ALL OF GRACE

It is, therefore, all of grace. Everything Paul is and possesses, is by the grace of God. Everything Apollos has and possesses is by the grace of God. This is true in a far deeper sense than usually understood. Do you realize that this is true of every last one of us. We are what we are, *not* by our own choice or volition, but by the grace of God. It would be difficult to find one single thing of which we can boast as something that we ourselves have achieved or acquired. Almost everything we are, physically, mentally, spiritually, was thrust upon us, wholly without our choice, before we had any voice in the matter whatsoever.

Physically, you are what you are, not by choice, but by birth. You came into this world without being consulted about your birth or anything about the condition in which you find yourself today. You were born with a body, in the choice of which you had no part. No one asked you whether you wanted to be black or white or yellow or red. No one asked you whom you wanted for your parents. You did not choose the country, the home, the environment in which you were to be born. No one asked you your choice of physique, whether tall or short, lean or fat. No one asked you what color of eyes or hair you wanted. In fact, your entire physical being was thrust upon you without your own knowledge or your own consent, or without any consultation with you. And while proper care of that body may determine health or sickness, strength or weakness, the basic characteristics of your physical being were all genetically determined at the moment of your conception. They are a matter of simple genetics, not of choice. Of our physical being it may be said:

Who maketh thee to differ from another? and what hast thou that thou didst not receive (I Corinthians 4:7).

If this be true, and it must be true, where then is our

boasting? Why be proud because we are physically superior to others? Indeed, it should humble us to realize that without our choice, God by His grace has given us the bodies that we do possess.

## MENTALLY TOO

Now what is true of the physical is true of the mental. Some people are born with normal mentality, others are born with inferior mental powers, others are idiots, and imbeciles. Some have bright minds, others dull, some are geniuses, others are morons. Over this also we had absolutely no control. We were born with these faculties fixed and unalterable from the day of our conception. Very true, our faculties may be trained and developed, but nothing more can be gotten out of a person than was born into that person. What we are mentally was not our fault, but it was all predetermined, wholly apart from anything we could do, even before we were born. Why then be proud and boast and strut, because by the grace of God we have been given a mentality which is superior to that of others?

## SPIRITUALLY ALSO

This truth of what we are, without any credit coming to us, or any choice on our part, regarding the physical and the mental, is just as true in an amazingly large measure regarding the spiritual blessings which the Lord has thrust upon us. If today you are saved, it was not because you were wiser or better, or had sense enough to believe the Gospel over and above others. Basically your conversion was the climax and result of a long train of circumstances and influences utterly beyond your control.

Why were you born in a Christian environment? Did you choose to be born in a Christian home? You might have been born in the heart of Africa and gone through life without ever even having heard the name of the Lord. Over these things you had absolutely no control, and had nothing to say. Were you consulted as to your choice of a place of birth? Were you born of Christian parents who perhaps early taught you the Word of God, and how to pray, and pointed you to the Lord Jesus Christ? You did not choose those parents. As far as your say in the matter is concerned, you might have been born in a savage, cannibalistic hut in the jungle. Did you choose to be born in a community where the Gospel was preached? We all know better than this, and so when we heard the Gospel and believed it, it was but the culmination of a long train of circumstances beyond our control, which were thrust upon us even before we were born, and over which we had absolutely nothing to say.

### GRACE, GRACE, GRACE

And so we see that everything we have is grace. Someone has aptly said, "Everything we have outside of hell is the grace of God." When we understand this wonderful truth of the grace of God, it is the end of all carnality, pride, and strife and division, and judging of our fellow men, and setting ourselves up as superior to others. Grace is the death of pride, it means an end to the works of the flesh. Grace puts us in the dust and teaches us to esteem our brother better than ourselves. Grace ends all strife and division, selfishness, boasting, and pride. Whenever I see a Christian, and especially a preacher, proud and overbearing, strutting and putting on airs, I just say to myself, "That man needs to know more of the grace of God."

Until we realize that we deserve nothing but hell, and have forfeited everything, and that we should glory only in the grace of God, we are still children in the faith and babes that need to be fed with milk instead of meat. Without understanding the grace of God, no one can be all that he should be for the Lord. Let these words, therefore, burn upon our hearts:

> For who maketh thee to differ from another? and what hast thou that thou didst not receive? now if thou didst receive it,

why dost thou glory, as if thou hadst not received it? (I Corinthians 4:7).

### UNFATHOMABLE GRACE

We will probably never understand fully the grace of God and all that is implied in the expression, "grace of God," until we reach the glory and see all of the circumstances which were brought to bear upon our lives, of which we are wholly unconscious now. What we are today is the result of circumstances, conditions and influences which began long before our birth, and even before our conception, and so the grace of God is to be the motive and the incentive for lives of service that will be pleasing unto Him. The grace of God excludes all merit and human worth, and puts us in the dust before the Lord can take us up. It is difficult to define the grace of God. All the words in all the languages of the world are inadequate to express fully what is implied in that term. And yet in the measure that we understand what the grace of God is in our lives, in that measure can our service be acceptable unto Him. The idea of grace has been expressed in the hymn by the late Dr. James M. Gray of the Moody Bible Institute:

> Naught have I gotten but what I received,
>   Grace hath bestowed it, since I have believed.
> Boasting excluded, pride I abase;
>   I'm only a sinner, saved by grace.
>
> Suffer a sinner, whose heart overflows,
>   Loving his Saviour, to tell what he knows;
> Once more to tell it, would I embrace,
>   I'm only a sinner, saved by grace.

And apart from this grace of God there is no salvation for anyone. As long as an individual feels that he has something of merit or worth or spiritual strength, he is not even a candidate for salvation. The Lord must first find the sinner in the dust, utterly hopeless and helpless before He is able to save him. Luke tells us in Luke 19:10 that "the Son of man is come to seek and to save that which was lost."

And Paul in I Timothy 1:15 says:

> This is a faithful saying, and worthy of all acceptation, that Christ Jesus came into the world to save sinners, of whom I am chief (I Timothy 1:15).

This is the message of the grace of God. It cannot be better expressed than Paul expresses it in his writing to the Corinthians, as he seeks to correct the sin of carnality, sectarianism, envying and strife, so prevalent in the Corinthian church. We, therefore, conclude this chapter with the words written by Paul himself:

> For by grace are ye saved through faith; and that not of yourselves: it is the gift of God:
> Not of works, lest any man should boast.
> For we are his workmanship, created in Christ Jesus unto good works, which God hath before ordained that we should walk in them (Ephesians 2:8-10).

This indeed is a humbling truth, and one hard for the proud heart of man to accept; yet there is no salvation except by the grace of God. Before we can become anything for Him, we must become nothing in ourselves. *When God creates a new thing, He always begins with nothing.*

*Chapter Nine*

## DISCIPLINE IN THE CHURCH

> It is reported commonly that there is fornication among you, and such fornication as is not so much as named among the Gentiles, that one should have his father's wife (I Corinthians 5:1).

IN the church at Corinth was a man who was openly living an incestuous life with his own step-mother. This was not a rumor; it was based on open knowledge and shameless publicity. It was common knowledge that this sin was indulged in by a member of the Christian assembly, but worse than this was the fact, that it was countenanced by the church without proper disciplinary action on the part of the assembly.

How Paul received this report we cannot state definitely. Perhaps the members of the household of Chloe, who had informed Paul of the carnality and sectarianism in the assembly (I Corinthians 2) had also told him of this unspeakable immoral situation in the church. Or it may have been reported to Paul in the letter written by members of the Corinthian assembly who were at a loss how to deal with this particular problem. Evidently Paul had received a letter from persons in the church at Corinth, deeply concerned about the spiritual condition of the assembly. In chapter 7, verse 1, Paul refers to this letter and says:

> Now concerning the things whereof ye wrote unto me: It is good for a man not to touch a woman (I Corinthians 7:1).

When Paul heard about these things, he sent Timothy to Corinth (I Corinthians 4:17) evidently to investigate the matter fully and to report all of the facts to him personally before he acted in the matter. Paul, therefore, did not act upon a mere rumor or pass judgment hastily, but only after the evidence was conclusive. And so he says:

> It is reported commonly that there is fornication among you (I Corinthians 5:1).

It was common knowledge among the people, and was a matter of public reproach. The word in the Greek is even stronger and could be translated "notorious," or "with absolute certainty." And only after determining all the facts does he bring up the matter. He was not judging a private sin, but a public scandal, and therefore speaks openly concerning it.

## SIN UNTO DEATH

The seriousness of this sin was greatly increased, because it was in open violation of the clear warning of Scripture in Deuteronomy 27:20:

> Cursed be he that lieth with his father's wife; because he uncovereth his father's skirt (Deuteronomy 27:20a).

It was a sin against better light, and therefore it comes under the classification of willful or presumptuous or premeditated sin. It was a sin which must be judged if necessary with the penalty of death. It was a "sin unto death."

Now notice the depth of the carnality to which the assembly at Corinth had sunk. They were so busy fighting, bickering, envying one another and splitting theological hairs, and arguing over personalities and ordinances and doctrines that they had paid no attention to this terrible immoral situation in their midst. And so Paul continues indignantly in verse 2:

> And ye are puffed up, and have not rather mourned, that he that hath done this deed might be taken away from among you.

What a tragically sad condition. The believers in Corinth were so blinded by carnality and spiritual pride, boasting of their own superiority, that they tolerated the grossest forms of immorality in their midst. This sin needed to be judged too, but it could hardly be done by those who themselves were carnal. And so Paul calls upon the church to deal with this matter officially.

Paul demands that this sin therefore be publically denounced and judged, and proper public action taken. Remember that this was a public sin. In the previous chapters Paul had been warning against Christians judging one another. In I Corinthians 4:5 Paul says:

> Therefore judge nothing before the time, until the Lord come, who both will bring to light the hidden things of darkness, and will make manifest the counsels of the hearts.

However, these instructions are against individual judgment of personal sins, where all the facts are not known. But in the case of this particular man in Corinth, and his stepmother, it was quite a different matter. This was a public sin, an open sin, an overt sin, and a reproach upon the cause of Christ, and injured the testimony of the entire assembly. The judgment of this sin, therefore, was not the business of any one individual, but was to be an action of the assembly as a whole. No church, no assembly has any right to tolerate open public sin in its membership without judging it according to the Word of God. And so Paul instructs them:

> In the name of our Lord Jesus Christ, when ye are gathered together, and my spirit, with the power of our Lord Jesus Christ,
> To deliver such an one unto Satan for the destruction of the flesh, that the spirit may be saved in the day of the Lord Jesus (I Corinthians 5:4, 5).

This indeed is strong medicine. They are to assemble in the name of the Lord Jesus Christ. This implies proper preparation in prayer and self-examination, and a confession of their own failure. Only in this way could they assemble "with the power of the Lord Jesus Christ."

Then they were publicly to separate this willfully, persistently, disobedient member from their fellowship. This did not mean that they considered him unsaved, or that they passed judgment on his salvation (which is never our business), but their action was for the good of the offender and for the testimony of the assembly and the church. The church is to exercise discipline, demanding public confession for public sin. Refusal to be corrected calls for discipline, disfellowshipping of the offending member, and turning him over to the chastening of the Lord. In II Thessalonians we read:

> Now we command you, brethren, in the name of our Lord Jesus Christ, that ye withdraw yourselves from every brother that walketh disorderly (II Thessalonians 3:6).

Notice that Paul is speaking of our responsibility toward an erring *brother*. It is not a matter of judging an unsaved man; that too is not our business. Because the wayward one is still a brother, we are to deal in discipline with him. Again Paul says in verse 14 of II Thessalonians 3:

> And if any man obey not our word by this epistle, note that man, and have no company with him, that he may be ashamed.
> Yet count him not as an enemy, but admonish him as a brother (II Thessalonians 3:14, 15).

Now in the case of the offender in this chapter in the church of Corinth, there evidently was no repentance, no confession, and so Paul calls for official action declaring this man to be separated from the assembly and, if he continues in his sin, to "deliver him unto Satan for the destruction of the flesh."

## DELIVERED UNTO SATAN

They were to stop praying for this man, and, under God, allow the Devil to put this man to death. This was a "sin unto death," and of such John says in I John 5:16:

> If any man see his brother sin a sin which is not unto death, he shall ask, and he shall give him life for them that sin not unto death. There is a sin unto death: I do not say that he shall pray for it (I John 5:16).

The Bible is crystal clear that God visits continued willful, deliberate, presumptuous disobedience on the part of His children with judgment and severe chastening. In I Corinthians 11 Paul says:

> But let a man examine himself, and so let him eat of that bread, and drink of that cup.
> For he that eateth and drinketh unworthily, eateth and

drinketh damnation [judgment] to himself, not discerning the Lord's body (I Corinthians 11:28, 29).

To refuse self-examination and self-judgment and to continue in willful sin against better light, calls for the judgment of God. And now will you notice the form that this judgment takes:

For this cause many are weak and sickly among you, and many sleep (I Corinthians 11:30).

God sends weakness and sickness upon His children in an effort to bring His children to repentance. And if this does not produce results, the Lord may even take that child home by the way of death. God would rather have His children taken out of this world by death, than to have them continue to live in willful disobedience. It does not, however, involve loss of salvation; it is for the purpose of correction. And so Paul continues:

For if we would judge ourselves, we should not be judged.
But when we are judged, we are chastened of the Lord, that we should not be condemned with the world (I Corinthians 11:31, 32).

### THE SPIRIT SAVED

So it was in the case of the incestuous brother in the church at Corinth. The assembly was to recognize this as "the sin unto death," break fellowship with him, cease praying for him, and turn him over to God for judgment. God could give permission to Satan to destroy this man by death, but farther than this Satan cannot go, for Paul adds: ". . . that the spirit may be saved in the day of the Lord Jesus" (I Corinthians 5:5b).

It seems from this passage that Satan is given power over the bodies even of believers by the permission of God, but he cannot touch their salvation. Praise God for that. Whether this man died soon after we are not told. It may be that like Ananias and Sapphira he was stricken dead.

We have another instance mentioned in I Timothy 1:20.

Here Paul warns Timothy against brethren who bring false doctrines, and says concerning them:

> Of whom is Hymenaeus and Alexander; whom I have delivered unto Satan, that they may learn not to blaspheme (I Timothy 1:20).

## THE APPLICATION

But before we close this chapter, may we apply this lesson to our own hearts. It is a serious thing to be a Christian. It is a tremendously serious thing to know God's Word, for we are expected to walk in the light of the knowledge which we possess and have been given by Him. To continue therefore in known and willful sin will bring God's chastening sooner or later. The chastening may take the form of sickness or weakness and even death. How important it is, therefore, that we as believers should examine our hearts daily and confess before the Lord every known and doubtful sin.

The question often arises, How may we know whether we have committed the sin unto death? This is an easy question to answer, for we believe that those who are guilty of the "sin unto death," which can only be corrected by the judgment of God, are those who have no concern and show no signs of repentance. If there is a consciousness of guilt and a real concern concerning our condition, and we are willing to repent and confess it before the Lord, then we may rest assured that we have not committed a "sin unto death." For His promise stands absolutely sure and steadfast:

> If we confess our sins, he is faithful and just to forgive us our sins, and to cleanse us from all unrighteousness (I John 1:9).

## Chapter Ten

# LAW SUITS AMONG THE SAINTS

Dare any of you, having a matter against another, go to law before the unjust, and not before the saints?

Do ye not know that the saints shall judge the world? and if the world shall be judged by you, are ye unworthy to judge the smallest matters?

Know ye not that we shall judge angels? how much more things that pertain to this life? (I Corinthians 6:1-3).

THE second specific error in the church at Corinth is now taken up by the apostle Paul after he has disposed of the matter of the brother in the assembly who had been living in open adultery. In chapter 5 he had instructed the saints in Corinth in the matter of disciplining a disorderly brother to safeguard the purity of the assembly. And now he takes up another serious matter. Brothers in Christ were going to the courts of law to settle their differences before the world. Just what the issues in Corinth were, over which they sued one another in the public courts, we are not told, neither does it make any difference. But we do know they were little, petty, insignificant matters which could easily have been taken care of if the love of Christ had only prevailed. This is perfectly evident, for Paul says in verse 2:

Are ye unworthy to judge the smallest matters? (I Corinthians 6:2b).

## FRUIT OF CARNALITY

Now this situation was another result of the carnality which was so characteristic of the Corinthian church. Paul had written in I Corinthians 3:3:

65

> For ye are yet carnal: for whereas there is among you envy-ing, and strife, and divisions, are ye not carnal, and walk as men? (I Corinthians 3:3).

The result of this envy and strife was division among the believers, and this division, called "sectarianism," arose over personalities and petty differences. And in the heat of the strife things were done and said which resulted in one member going to the courts of law and suing another brother before the world — not over important matters, but says Paul "the smallest matters."

## TRAGEDY IN THE CHURCH

And this is the awful tragic result of sectarianism and carnality. The great majority of squabbles and fights and divisions among believers are not usually over important matters of doctrine or even of conduct at all, but they are all too often over childish, petty, picayune things, things of so little consequence that they are silly in themselves. If the controversy is a matter of heresy and serious false doctrine, or gross immorality, of course it must be dealt with as we have seen in the previous chapter. We have seen that gross immorality must be severely dealt with, even to the extent of delivering the offender over to death. But all too often it is not over any serious matter that Christians differ, but rather over matters of personality and minor interpretation, and theological hair-splitting. How many of the "splits" in funda-mental circles are for the good cause of serious doctrinal error or immorality? In most cases they are over some petty insult or personal hurt. Someone's pride has been hurt, some-one has been neglected, someone talked about someone else, and the fight is on, and grows and grows and grows until it ends up in the courts.

## THE REMEDY

Now notice Paul's argument. He says:

> Dare any of you, having a matter against another, go to law before the unjust [the world], and not before the saints? (I Corinthians 6:1).

Are you so carnal and so fleshly, so puerile, so childish, so immature that you cannot settle these little insignificant differences among yourselves without dragging them out as a spectacle before all the world? How sad and tragic it is that we cannot keep our family troubles to ourselves. How deplorable, that when a situation develops in the church it is immediately plastered on the front page of the public newspaper and heralded over the telephone, with all of its reproach on the testimony of the Lord Jesus Christ.

### JUDGE ANGELS

You, says Paul, who will someday sit in judgment upon the world and even upon the angels [presumably fallen angels], can't you even settle these little differences among yourselves? And then Paul engages in a bit of bitter, biting sarcasm.

> If then ye have judgments of things pertaining to this life, set them to judge who are least esteemed in the church (I Corinthians 6:4).

The word "esteemed" is a strong word. Those who are least esteemed means literally those who are "contemptible," who are "despised," and who count among you for nothing. This is divine sarcasm and apostolic irony. What, says Paul: "Is it so, that there is not a wise man among you? no, not one that shall be able to judge between his brethren?" (I Corinthians 6:5).

Isn't there a single individual in the entire church who has wisdom and sane judgment enough to bring the two offending parties together? Listen, says Paul, if you were spiritual, if you had the grace of Christ, the lowest, the most despised, most ignorant saint, the least esteemed in the church, would know the answer to your problem. But instead:

> Brother goeth to law with brother, and that before the unbelievers (I Corinthians 6:6).

The world sets even a better example than some Christians. When a dispute arises among different factions, such as, for instance, capital and labor, and they reach an impasse, they will submit their grievance to an appointed impartial board of arbitration and if they have good sense they abide by the decision of that board. Paul refers to something of this nature. When differences arise, don't blaze it abroad says Paul. Keep it within the circle of the family. Set some of the least esteemed of the brethren to judge the situation, with the agreement that the offending parties will abide by the decision. This would once for all end the habit of dragging the thing before the world and the public eye.

### Why The Least Esteemed?

We may here ask the question, Why call on the "least esteemed," the most insignificant members of the assembly to judge, and not call upon the leaders and the prominent ones in the church? Why not the board of deacons? Because these "least esteemed brethren" were probably the poorer members who counted for but little, who didn't have many friends and didn't have any personal prejudices. They would not be apt to favor one above the other. They had nothing to lose in the way of prestige or position or friends. Set these who are least esteemed to judge over these matters. Let them hear both sides and give their counsel.

### The Big Problem

But this brings up a tremendous problem. Suppose one or both parties are unwilling to abide by this Scriptural procedure. Then it becomes a matter of church action. If a brother remains stubborn, and unwilling to abide by this divinely inspired solution, the assembly can take action and disfellowship the unruly brother according to the rules laid down in chapter 5 in the case of the man continuing in his immoral life. If one or the other then still goes to law, he must be disciplined and if need be separated from the fellowship of the believers. To condone such acts because of the position or the influence or the wealth of the offender is permanently to cripple the testimony of the Church of the living God.

## THE REAL VICTORY

Notice Paul's direct answer to the problem in verse 7:

> Now therefore there is utterly a fault among you, because ye go to law one with another. Why do ye not rather take wrong? why do ye not rather suffer yourselves to be defrauded?
> Nay, ye do wrong, and defraud, and that your brethren (I Corinthians 6:7, 8).

The word translated "defraud" means to "deprive of." It may refer to money, but not necessarily to material possessions The same word is used in chapter 7, verse 5, in speaking of the intimate conjugal relationship of husbands and wives, in the words:

> Defraud ye not one the other, except it be with consent for a time, that ye may give yourselves to fasting and prayer; and come together again, that Satan tempt you not for your incontinency [testimony] (I Corinthians 7:5).

Here the word "defraud" refers to depriving one another of the normal God-given privileges of married life.

And so we are only left to guess what particular case Paul had in mind. It refers to depriving a brother of that which he has a right to expect, whether it be the payment of a debt or some other obligation.

## THE TRIUMPH OF GRACE

And now comes the bitter pill, hard for the flesh to swallow. Paul says, Rather than go to law, rather than assert your rights, rather than stand upon your just claims; be willing to be the least, no matter what the cost may be. Suffer wrong, and then forget about it. Take the loss if need be, rather than bring reproach on the cause of the Lord Jesus Christ. Your testimony and the testimony of the church is worth far more, is far more important than all the other things in the world. God will honor your subjection to His will and His Word, and He will make it all up to you in the end, if you dare to be obedient and the least. The brother who refuses to pay you what you legally have coming is the loser. If you are willing to suffer loss for the sake of Christ and your testimony, you are the gainer. It will all be thrashed out at the Judgment Seat of Christ.

### NOT FOR THE WORLD

Now all of this of course is for believers only, for Paul is dealing in I Corinthians only with those who have been born again and belong to the Lord Jesus. What he has to say in this connection therefore is not for the world, and has no application to those who are unconverted. For we cannot expect the world to abide by the Word of God, which they do not believe, or to obey Him, whom they have not accepted. It does not mean, therefore, that a Christian in business has no right to go to law with the world to safeguard his interests and property in the collection of debts and protection of his holdings. That is quite another matter. We as Christians have a right to call in the police when threatened, and take legal action against other attacks upon our person, our liberties, or our possessions. God has constituted these authorities and these things for our use and for our protection.

But among believers, fellow members of the body of Christ, it should never even be considered. Our example there is the Lord Jesus Christ.

> Who, when he was reviled, reviled not again; when he suffered, he threatened not; but committed himself to him that judgeth righteously:
>
> By whose stripes ye were healed (I Peter 2:23, 24b).

We might well take heed to the words of Paul when he says:

> Let this mind be in you, which was also in Christ Jesus:
>
> Who, being in the form of God, thought it not robbery to be equal with God:
>
> But made himself of no reputation, and took upon him the form of a servant, and was made in the likeness of men:
>
> And being found in fashion as a man, he humbled himself, and became obedient unto death, even the death of the cross.

Wherefore God also hath highly exalted him, and given him a name which is above every name:

That at the name of Jesus every knee should bow, of things in heaven, and things in earth, and things under the earth;

And that every tongue should confess that Jesus Christ is Lord (Philippians 2:5-11).

This is the Christian pattern, this is God's will, and this is the path of blessing — walk ye therefore in it. To disobey is to place yourself in the way of the chastening of the Lord. We conclude this chapter, therefore, by repeating Paul's words:

Why do ye not rather take wrong? why do ye not rather suffer yourselves to be defrauded?

Nay, ye do wrong, and defraud, and that your brethren (I Corinthians 6:7, 8).

Finally, we must again emphasize the fact that the body is greater than any one member, and the members are subject to the head. It is not, therefore, a question of personal wrong, but a question of what effect upon the testimony of the Lord Jesus Christ a particular action may have. In all of these things we are to consider what effect our action will have upon the person of our Lord, and what it will do to the witness of the fellowship of believers.

## Chapter Eleven

# HUSBANDS AND WIVES

> Now concerning the things whereof ye wrote unto me: It is good for a man not to touch a woman.
>
> Nevertheless, to avoid fornication, let every man have his own wife, and let every woman have her own husband.
>
> Let the husband render unto the wife due benevolence: and likewise also the wife unto the husband (I Corinthians 7:1-3).

THE church at Corinth was a church of contradictions. It was a church of extreme opposites. While there were those who made the grace of God and their liberty in Christ an excuse for living in sin, there were others who went to the opposite extreme of legality, and advocated asceticism and total withdrawal from the world, and all the ordinary innocent necessities of life. They counted every physical thing as evil, and taught and practiced abstinence and continency to the point of foolish asceticism. With the former group, who made the grace of God an excuse for all kinds of looseness and immorality and sin, Paul had dealt with in the preceding chapters. But now he is to deal with the other extreme which was present in the Corinthian church. While one group held marriage very lightly and abused its privileges, making their liberty a cloak for lasciviousness, there were others who denounced marriage as something to be studiously avoided, as something fleshly and sensual. They took a position of extreme asceticism and fanaticism. They objected to the conjugal relationship of husband and wife. They were indignant in their extreme reaction against the laxity of others, but made the mistake of themselves going to the opposite extreme.

And while they considered others who went to immoral extremes as sinful and evil, they seemed to forget that asceticism also has its evils and its drawbacks. And so they advocated celibacy and taught that there was more virtue in the unmarried state than in the marriage relationship.

The controversy waxed so hot that they decided to write to Paul about the matter because they were unable to come to any decision among themselves.

## CONDITIONS ALTER CIRCUMSTANCES

No hard and fast rule is laid down by the apostle Paul, but he insists that the question is a matter of personal decision, and that one cannot legislate for, or judge his brother for thinking differently. "Let every man be persuaded in his own mind." If a man feels that he can serve the Lord better in the single state and is able to live a continent life, well and good. Paul himself was an example of this very thing, and says in I Corinthians 7:1:

It is good [all right] for a man not to touch a woman.

But, this was not by commandment but by permission, and just because you are able to be happy in the single state, do not make your personal experience a rule for others, do not make your own ideas the measuring stick and the only rule and guide for everyone else who may be differently constituted in temperament than you are. All men are not alike in their dispositions or in their sexual make-up. Some individuals are more highly sexed than others. This is no fault of theirs, nor is it a fault in itself. Sex in itself is never a sin. Sex is neither moral nor immoral. It is the abuse of this God-given function and faculty which makes it immoral.

The matter of marriage, therefore, is a personal matter to be decided by the individual, in his own circumstances, with his own individual disposition and physical constitution. In general God expects men and women to marry. He said in the beginning:

> It is not good that the man should be alone; I will make him an help-meet for him (Genesis 2:18).

Male and female God created the human race. The man and the woman were made for each other and the one complements the other. The one is incomplete without the other. God said:

> They shall be *one* flesh (Genesis 2:24b).

A husband and a wife therefore, constitute *one,* and one is composed of two halves. The unmarried state, therefore, is an incomplete state according to God's original purpose in creation.

### PERSONAL PRIVILEGE

But there are exceptions to this rule. It is not mandatory that all should marry, and so Paul says:

> It is good for a man not to touch a woman.
> Nevertheless, to avoid fornication, let every man have his own wife, and let every woman have her own husband (I Corinthians 7:1, 2).

God knows and understands how man was created with the desire for conjugal fellowship and the pure desire for children in the family and has made provision in the married state for this holy and beautiful exercise. This then is the rule, and the exceptions are individual personal matters.

### MORE SERIOUS

But this teaching of certain ascetics in Corinth who advocated celibacy and the virtue of the unmarried state had even more serious implications. They not only taught that it was a superior virtue to remain unmarried and continent, but they even advocated that married couples, husbands and wives live as though they were not married. They inferred that the normal intimate physical relationship of husbands and wives was sinful and evil and therefore demanded total abstinence from the God-given, God-created privilege of conjugal relationship.

This we may readily infer from what Paul deals with next in this chapter:

> Let the husband render unto the wife due benevolence: and likewise also the wife unto the husband (I Corinthians 7:3).

The verse freely translated would be:

> Let the husband regard the rights of his wife, and give her what is due her as a wife; and likewise the wife to her husband (I Corinthians 7:3).

There is no virtue in supposing that the most intimate function of married life is sinful. To the pure, all things are pure. It is indeed a sad, sad situation that the high and holy function of sex life should have been so abused that we have come to think of it as something filthy, sinful, and evil, something to be avoided; whereas in its proper use and place, —used as God intended it—it is the highest expression of oneness and intimacy with which the marriage relationship is endowed. We must speak of these things with restraint and apology, and are made to feel guilty when we speak of these things publicly, because of the onus which has been attached to sex by the abuse of it on the part of men and women. We must carefully choose our words when we speak on matters of this kind because of the evil associated with sex, through its abuse, in the minds of the average individual. And even then we shall be criticized and accused of being vulgar and offensive. To all such let me say in the words of Paul,

> Unto the pure all things are pure: but unto them that are defiled and unbelieving is nothing pure; but even their mind and conscience is defiled (Titus 1:15).

No, says the apostle Paul, there is no evil in the normal exercise of all the functions and privileges of married life. But such exercise must be by mutual love. It must transcend and originate in a higher motive than mere physical contact. Love between husband and wife will determine all their actions. The husband seeks to please the wife, the wife to please the husband. Each is willing to forego his or her personal wishes, if need be, for the sake of the other. And when this is done in Christian love, marriage can be beautiful.

Paul says that if each seeks to please the other, then true happiness can result, not in denying our God-given faculties, but exercising them for the God-given purpose of glorifying Him and of enjoying one another.

> The wife hath not power of her own body, but the husband: and likewise also the husband hath not power of his own body, but the wife (I Corinthians 7:4).

And so Paul continues in I Corinthians 7:5:

> Defraud ye not one the other, except it be with consent for a time, that ye may give yourselves to fasting and prayer; and come together again, that Satan tempt you not for your incontinency (I Corinthians 7:5).

### DEFRAUD YE NOT ONE THE OTHER

The word used in this verse and translated "defraud" may be rendered "deprive." However, there are special occasions when an interruption of the normal life of a husband and wife may become necessary and advisable. In times of great stress, in times of bereavement, in times of sorrow, in times of sickness, or when physical conditions demand it, there is virtue in temporary continence. But it must be by common mutual consent, and only for a time, lest Satan take advantage of either one or the other and tempt them to sin by their incontinency.

This is sound and inspired advice coming through the Holy Spirit by the apostle Paul. Marriage, first of all, is for fellowship and only secondarily for procreation. The fellowship expresses itself in many, many ways and is climaxed in the exercise of procreation and the rearing of a family for the glory of God. To restrain these normal functions may increase the strain rather than to subdue it. Childless marriages, therefore, have their problems and their difficulties which are utterly unknown in the families where children are normally born. And so Paul states that unnatural, unnecessary repressions of the normal functions which God has permitted only tend to increase rather than to diminish sinful temptations. Paul concludes his argument with the repeated advice that it is a matter of individual responsibility, or as he puts it:

> But I speak this by permission, and not of commandment (I Corinthians 7:6).

This is not a hard and fast rule, no one can lay hard and fast rules for each individual. Only the general principles can be laid down, and the individual application must be left to the personal decision of each one. And so Paul says:

> But I speak this by permission . . . and let every man be persuaded in his own mind (I Corinthians 7:6, Romans 14:5b).

Now the apostle Paul himself was an exception to the general rule. As far as we know he was a single man and felt that in his unmarried state he could be just as pleasing to God as if he had been married. But he would not impose this upon anyone else but he says further:

> For I would that all men were even as I myself. But every man hath his proper gift of God, one after this manner, and another after that.
> I say therefore to the unmarried and widows. It is good for them if they abide even as I.
> But if they cannot contain, let them marry; for it is better to marry than to burn (I Corinthians 7:7-9).

We are individually, therefore, responsible to God in the whole matter of living a life pleasing to Him. It is possible to establish a home which is a picture of heaven here upon the earth and a reflection of the relationship which exists in the Trinity between the Father, Son, and Holy Spirit, and also that which exists between the Head of the Body, Christ — the Bridegroom, and the Body — the Church the Bride of the Lord Jesus Christ. Thus God intended it to be in the beginning and thus it should ever be among believers. There is no question that the moral decay and awful corruption in these days comes from the breakdown of the ideal Christian Bible home, and the abuse of marriage for something other than fellowship and the rearing of a Christian family.

Before concluding this message on this rather intimate and touchy subject, we would again emphasize the fact that the primary purpose for which the marriage state was instituted was for mutual help and fellowship. The first statement we have in the Word of God is:

It is not good that the man should be alone (Genesis 2:18a).

We, therefore, see that even before the matter of procreation there is a deeper spiritual purpose in the married state, and this is for mutual helpfulness and for mutual fellowship. God distinctly said:

It is not good that the man should be alone; I will make him an help-meet for him (Genesis 2:18).

And when the marriage contract is consummated with only one purpose in mind, the fact that it is primarily for fellowship and mutual loving relationship which will make it easier for the man and woman to serve the Lord together than in the single state, that marriage will be a success.

And the only way such a family can be sure of the blessing of the Lord and prevent the corruption and the decay which ultimately must mean the corruption and the decay of the entire society of which the family is the unit, is to place Christ at the Head of the home, to acknowledge His will, and to bow immediately before His Word. As we have brought these messages we are calling upon each of you to examine your own lives and to measure your conduct in the home, in the family as husbands and wives, as fathers and mothers of children, by the standards which the Lord Himself has laid down. Then and then only can we expect the blessing of the Lord and meet Him with confidence at His appearing.

## Chapter Twelve

# SEPARATION AND DIVORCE

> And unto the married I command, yet not I, but the Lord,
> Let not the wife depart from her husband:
> But and if she depart, let her remain unmarried, or be
> reconciled to her husband: and let not the husband put away
> his wife (I Corinthians 7:10, 11).

ONE of the most vexing problems in the church at Corinth
was the matter of the unequal yoke in the marriage relationship. We must remember that these Christians were mostly
saved out of paganism, and in many cases one of the two
had come to the Lord Jesus Christ while the other remained
unsaved. Under Paul's preaching wives had been saved,
while the husbands remained unconverted, and vice versa.
This brought up the question of what the saved one was to
do. Some seemed to justify separation, on the grounds of the
unequal yoke. Others advised that husband and wife remain together. The Corinthians had evidently written to
Paul for his counsel and advice. Undoubtedly this was part
of the reason for the divisions and bickering, the contention
and the strife, and the separation which was so prevalent in
the church at Corinth. In order to solve this problem they
had therefore appealed to the apostle Paul for his verdict.

## Do Not Leave

The answer of Paul is in the form of a command. This
is unusual for Paul, who usually pleads with his audience on
the basis of the grace of God. His usual method of address-

ing them is: "I beseech you." But here he departs from this customary approach and says:

> I command [you] (I Corinthians 7:10a).

And then adds:

> Yet not I, but the Lord (I Corinthians 7:10b).

He emphasizes the fact that this is an inviolable rule. It is important to note the emphasis, therefore, of these words. It is as if Paul says, There are no exceptions to this rule. This is a matter not to be trifled with, for it is a thing of unusual seriousness, and therefore comes in the form of a command directly from the Lord. And here is the command:

> Let not the wife depart from her husband (I Corinthians 7:10b).

Clear and simple and unmistakable is the command. In the hope of winning him to Christ, the wife is to remain with her unsaved husband no matter what the cost may be or how difficult and unpleasant it may become. Then, too, if there be children in the home, it is a serious thing to break up that relationship and place upon them the stigma of a divorce and a broken home.

### ONLY ONE REASON

However, there is one cause for which divorce is permitted in the Scriptures. It is for the one sin of adultery. The Bible recognizes this, and this only, and none other, as a reason for divorce. And so Paul says:

> But and if she depart [assuming it is for the one scriptural cause of divorce, unfaithfulness] let her remain unmarried, or be reconciled to her husband (I Corinthians 7:11).

It seems that comment here is almost entirely unnecessary even though it is rejected by so many. The statement is direct and clear and unmistakable. If the offended party in marriage has grace enough to forgive the unfaithfulness of his or her mate, this is the desirable and commendable thing to do, and will be blessed of the Lord. But the offended party may obtain a divorce if he or she will, but only on the ground of unfaithfulness. The Bible recognizes no such grounds as incompatibility, mental cruelty, nonsupport, drunkenness or any other reason. We shall see why this is so a little farther on.

But in case divorce is resorted to, under no circumstances is the divorced believer to remarry while the other party to the divorce is still alive. Here is the simple statement:

> Let her remain unmarried, or be reconciled to her husband (I Corinthians 7:11).

Remarriage would close the door forever to a possible reconciliation, and reconciliation is the desirable thing. Maybe the guilty one would be saved, and the home could be restored again, and the stigma of separation be removed.

## ANOTHER SERIOUS PROBLEM

And now we take up the matter of desertion. Remember the problem in Corinth was one of mixed marriages between believers and unbelievers. It was not always a matter of unfaithfulness on the part of either one of the mates, but simply a matter of incompatibility in their faith. One was still a pagan, the other had become a Christian. The question was this: Has a believer who is married to an unbeliever a right to leave the unconverted mate? The answer follows:

> But to the rest speak I, not the Lord: If any brother hath a wife that believeth not, and she be pleased to dwell with him, let him not put her away.
>
> And the woman which hath an husband that believeth not, and if he be pleased to dwell with her, let her not leave him (I Corinthians 7:12, 13).

The believer, therefore, should never under any circumstances leave his or her unbelieving husband or wife. (As long as the unconverted mate is willing to dwell with the believer, no separation should ever be sought.) Of course, this may involve a great deal of sorrow, and tears, and heartache, and disappointment, and sacrifice, but there is one overwhelming reason why it should be endured. And this is stated in verse 14:

> For the unbelieving husband is sanctified by the wife, and the unbelieving wife is sanctified by the husband: else were

> your children unclean; but now are they holy (I Corinthians 7:14).

This much misunderstood and misinterpreted text must be looked at in the light of the context. The words "sanctified" and "holy" as used in this verse do not imply "salvation" in any sense whatsoever. Certainly a husband is not saved simply because he is married to a believer. The word "sanctify" means rather that a husband who lives with a saved person is in a place of special privilege, and in contact with influences which may later lead to his salvation. If the home be broken up, he is removed from this privilege and this influence and place of sanctified relationship. The same is true of the statement:

> Else were your children unclean; but now are they holy (I Corinthians 7:14b).

Certainly this does not mean that children are saved just because they have a believing father or mother. And certainly this has not the remotest reference to the sprinkling of babies. If the children are holy in the sense of being saved because of the believing parent, then also an unbelieving husband or wife is saved because of marriage to a believer. For says Paul:

> For the unbelieving husband is sanctified by the wife (I Corinthians 7:14a).

You see the teaching that little children are saved because of their birth from believing parents would then also mean that the marriage of an unbeliever to a believer would automatically make the unbeliever a Christian. However, Paul is thinking of the possibilities and the probabilities of the unbeliever's being saved, so that the home can be kept together, and can be prevented from being broken up. Notice carefully how Paul makes this clear:

> For what knowest thou, O wife, whether thou shalt save thy husband? or how knowest thou, O man, whether thou shalt save thy wife? (I Corinthians 7:16).

Remain together, therefore, in order that your contact may

result in their ultimate salvation. As long as you live with the unbelieving mate you can influence him or her for Christ, but once you are separated your influence is cut off immediately and permanently. So in the hope of winning him or her for Christ, stay with your unbelieving husband or wife, and the same goes for the children in the home. This is implied in the statement:

> Else were your children unclean; but now are they holy (I Corinthians 7:14).

As long as the home is not broken up your children are in the place of privilege and can be influenced for Christ, but when the home is broken and separation takes place, and the children go with the unbeliever, your chance of winning them for Christ is entirely gone. And even if the children should remain with you, the believing party, the probability of winning them for Christ would be reduced by their memory of the disagreement of their parents and the stigma of a divorce upon them. Statistics reveal the tremendous importance of a united home. The number of children who are saved from united homes is much larger than the number saved from the homes of divorced parents. It is a matter of simple statistics that most delinquent children come from broken homes where husband and wife have argued, and quibbled, and fought until a separation took place.

## ANOTHER PROBLEM

Of course, if the unbeliever deserts the believer there is nothing the believer can do. This is also clear from the words of Paul in verse 15:

> But if the unbelieving depart, let him depart. A brother or a sister is not under bondage in such cases: but God hath called us to peace (I Corinthians 7:15).

There are those who make this verse an argument for a remarriage of divorced people when they point to the statement that a brother or a sister is "not in bondage" in such cases. But this argument is negated entirely by the other statement of Paul in which he says:

> But and if she depart, let her remain unmarried, or be reconciled to her husband (I Corinthians 7:11).

We cannot build a doctrine on one isolated passage of Scripture.

### IMPORTANT LESSON

If these inspired words of the apostle Paul were heeded today they would solve many, many problems in the home. First of all, a believer should never marry an unbeliever. If this rule were obeyed much sorrow would be eliminated before it could begin. But it still is God's will that the believer should stick it out with her or his unbelieving mate, in the hope that the unbeliever may ultimately be saved, and for the sake of the influence upon the children in the home. Paul concludes his argument with an appeal to be faithful in the place where you happen to find yourself when you are saved.

> But as God hath distributed to every man, as the Lord hath called every one, so let him walk. And so ordain I in all churches.
>
> Is any man called being circumcised? let him not become uncircumcised. Is any called in uncircumcision? let him not be circumcised.
>
> Circumcision is nothing, and uncircumcision is nothing, but the keeping of the commandments of God (I Corinthians 7: 17-19).

The commandments of God here referred to are the commandments which Paul has just laid down regarding the duty of the believer not to seek separation from the unbeliever. They have nothing to do with the Ten Commandments at all. This is immediately evident from what follows:

> Let every man abide in the same calling wherein he was called.
>
> Art thou called being a servant? care not for it: but if thou mayest be made free, use it rather.
>
> For he that is called in the Lord, being a servant, is the Lord's freeman: likewise also he that is called, being free, is Christ's servant.

> Ye are bought with a price; be not ye the servants of men (I Corinthians 7:20-23).

And on this argument he seeks to admonish the Corinthian believers to remain in the state wherein they find themselves.

Are you the victim of an unhappy marriage? Are you, either because of your own mistake in marrying an unbeliever, or because you were saved after you were married involved in a divided home? Does it sometimes seem unbearable to go on any longer? We certainly sympathize with you and we are not treating the situation lightly by any means, but seeing that eternity is at stake for the members of your family who may yet be unsaved, we have only one advice to give on the basis of Scripture, and that is to bear your burden patiently. Do not increase your judgment by seeking the easy way out, but pray for God's grace to bear your burden and claim your unsaved loved ones for the Lord Jesus. Pray that your home will be united in Christ, and together you can claim your children for the Lord. Oh, believer, think twice and pray thrice before you act in haste, only to repent at leisure. The easy way out may well be the wrong way out. No matter what sacrifice may be required of you, if it results in salvation of your loved ones and your children it will be worth it all.

> And unto the married I command, yet not I, but the Lord, let not the wife depart from her husband:
>
> But and if she depart, let her remain unmarried, or be reconciled to her husband: and let not the husband put away his wife (I Corinthians 7:10, 11).

## Chapter Thirteen

# TO MARRY OR NOT TO MARRY?

Now concerning virgins I have no commandment of the Lord: yet I give my judgment, as one that hath obtained mercy of the Lord to be faithful.

I suppose therefore that this is good for the present distress, I say, that it is good for a man so to be.

Art thou bound unto a wife? seek not to be loosed. Art thou loosed from a wife? seek not a wife.

But and if thou marry, thou hast not sinned; and if a virgin marry, she hath not sinned. Nevertheless such shall have trouble in the flesh: but I spare you (I Corinthians 7:25-28).

IN these verses Paul repeats what he has said in the preceding verses. He advises his followers to remain in the state in which they find themselves during the distress which was prevalent in the days when the epistle was written. In order to understand these strange and difficult instructions of Paul, we must transport ourselves back to the time in which Paul wrote. They were days of great stress and persecution and opposition from the enemy. The Christians were despised and suspected on every hand. They were subjected to the greatest acts of violence and even to death. In view of all this Paul says to the unmarried: Remain as you are because of the uncertainty of these terrible days of persecution. And then too, they were evidently looking for the imminent return of the Lord Jesus Christ. The persecutions they endured were regarded by them as the persecutions predicted as coming just before the return of the Saviour, and in view of His early return (which they evidently expected), Paul gives the following advice:

If married remain so, if single remain single.

Listen to his words as given in this chapter:

> But this I say, brethren, the time is short: it remaineth, that both they that have wives be as though they had none;
>
> And they that weep, as though they wept not; and they that rejoice: as though they rejoiced not; and they that buy, as though they possessed not;
>
> And they that use this world, as not abusing it: for the fashion of this world passeth away (I Corinthians 7:29-31).

Now the force of these words is unmistakable. So terrible were the days in which Paul wrote, and so severe was the persecution, and Paul so imminently expected the return of Christ for His own that he pleads with them to be more occupied with spiritual things than with the material, more concerned with eternal matters than with temporal. Put first things first, he seems to say, and let all earthly matters be secondary. And the reason is that they might have victory and be ready to meet Him when He comes. And so he says:

> But I would have you without carefulness [cares of this world]. He that is unmarried careth for the things that belong to the Lord, how he may please the Lord:
>
> But he that is married careth for the things that are of the world, how he may please his wife.
>
> There is difference also between a wife and a virgin. The unmarried woman careth for the things of the Lord, that she may be holy both in body and in spirit: but she that is married careth for the things of the world, how she may please her husband.
>
> And this I speak for your own profit; not that I may cast a snare upon you, but for that which is comely, and that ye may attend upon the Lord without distraction (I Corinthians 7:32-35).

Now these verses again must be placed in the setting of the time in which Paul was writing. They cannot be promiscuously applied to every situation. In view of the conditions of Paul's day he gives this advice. And notice that it was in the form of advice and not in the form of a commandment, for he hastens to make clear in verse 35:

> And this I speak for your own profit; not that I may cast a snare upon you [not by way of restraint], but for that which is comely [permissible], and that ye may attend upon the Lord without distraction (I Corinthians 7:35).

The word distraction means "cares." Paul would spare the believers unnecessary "cares of this life" in view of the local circumstances which prevailed in that day.

### Concerning Virgins

But all of this is a matter of personal decision. How gracious Paul is in his respect for the personal opinions and ideas of each individual in these difficult matters. He lays down no hard and fast rule by way of commandment, but recognizes that what would be wise for one, might be extremely unwise for another. Listen to Paul's gracious approach to the matter:

> But if any man think that he behaveth himself uncomely toward his virgin, if she pass the flower of her age, and need so require, let him do what he will, he sinneth not: let them marry.
>
> Nevertheless he that standeth stedfast in his heart, having no necessity, but hath power over his heart that he will keep his virgin, doeth well.
>
> So then he that giveth her in marriage doeth well; but he that giveth her not in marriage doeth better (I Corinthians 7:36-38).

It was the custom in ancient times for the father to choose the husband for his daughter. No marriage was countenanced without the consent of the father of the girl involved. In many instances the bride was chosen exclusively by the father (for example, Abraham's choice of a bride for Isaac). Today we have a faint reflection of this custom when the prospective groom goes through the formality of asking a father for the hand of his daughter in marriage. But today that practice has become a mere formality. If the father says no, the couple just elope and get married anyway.

But not so in the days of Paul. The father must give the bride in marriage and it must always be with his full consent. But if the father thinks that refusal to let her marry after she has passed the flower of her age may be misinterpreted or bring scandal upon her and her suitor, then let them marry. The phrase "flower of her age" means maturity or "of age." It means that if the virgin daughter is of marriageable age, usually considered among the ancients as about twenty years, although there is no age set in the Scriptures, then she is eligible for marriage. But if there is no necessity, no urgent reason, and in view of present circumstances the father decides against marriage, he does no wrong, and the obedient daughter abides by the decision of the father. It is quite difficult to apply all this to our own present age, to which these ideas are so foreign, unless we remember the circumstances of stress and persecution which prevailed in Corinth when Paul wrote all of this. Elsewhere and under other conditions, entirely different advice might have been given.

## MARRIAGE PERMANENT

However, the advice Paul gives is a solemn warning against regarding lightly the marriage relationship between husbands and wives. It is a solemn rebuke against hasty marriages. Marriage is a solemn affair and a very serious thing and should be entered into only with the full knowledge of its responsibilities as well as its privileges. It is not a temporary arrangement, but is according to the Scripture an absolute contract for life. This seems to be in the mind of Paul also, for he concludes this section rather abruptly with the reminder:

> The wife is bound by the law as long as her husband liveth; but if her husband be dead, she is at liberty to be married to whom she will; only in the Lord (I Corinthians 7:39).

The only thing, therefore, which can dissolve the relationship between Christian husbands and wives is death. Marriage is a contract for life. In the matters concerning the advisability of marriage there is individual latitude of opinion. There is no added virtue either in the married or in the unmarried state, but once marriage has been consummated and contracted, nothing can dissolve it but death of one of the parties. They have become one flesh. The husband has become the head of the wife, and the wife has become the body of the head. A marital monstrosity of a two-headed body is unthinkable in the mind of Paul. And this is just exactly what a remarriage of a divorced person would constitute.

Marriage, therefore, in the sight of God is a permanent arrangement, and it is for the duration of temporal life. "For better, for worse, for richer, for poorer and forsaking every other, cleave to her only as long as you both shall live" was the vow you took when you were united. Nothing but sorrow and heartache can result from breaking this solemn promise which is a vow before Almighty God.

Or perhaps you are contemplating marriage. I speak only to believers, to born-again Christians. This is not for the unsaved, for they do not believe the Word of God, neither are subject to the law of God. But we speak to believers, just as Paul wrote in I Corinthians only to those who had been born-again. If you are a believer and are contemplating marriage, then before you go through with it remember these things:

1. Marriage with an unbeliever is strictly forbidden by the Word of God. To this rule there are no exceptions.

2. Once you are married there is no going back without inviting the judgment of Almighty God.

3. When you marry you surrender your individual will in seeking first not your own desires, but first of all how you may please your mate. Your will becomes the will of another, and you surrender your own desires and inclinations to the will of the one whom you have chosen to marry.

4. Marriage is not for the gratification of fleshly desire by mere physical contact alone, but for a relationship of fellowship and a responsibility of rearing a family for God. For these two purposes God has instituted marriage. First for fellowship, and secondly for the rearing of a family.

5. Christ must be enthroned as the Head of the house. Mutually dedicate your lives as husband and wife to Him before you marry. Pray and pray together to know His will. If you as believing lovers have not prayed together over your proposed marriage, you better postpone it until together you have sought the will of the Lord for your lives and for your married relationship.

Post these simple rules over your kitchen table and read them every day and it will save you much sorrow and sadness, I assure you.

If these rules were earnestly considered and faithfully carried out, they would end a great deal of sadness and heartache and distress among the believers who have entered too hastily into the marriage relationship. We believe with all of our hearts that there is one man and one woman designed by God to live together and establish a Christian home. Of course when this relationship is dissolved by death, remarriage is justified; but we do believe that God directs men and women to come together. However, if we go ahead on our own inclinations without seeking the will of the Lord, it may result in tragedy, even in the lives where two believers have been mutually joined together. All of the sadness in the homes is not due to mixed marriages, but a great deal of it is due to lack of preparation and failure to seek the will of the Lord before entry into marriage. Aside from your conversion to the Lord Jesus, there is no more important step that any man or any woman can take than the marriage relationship. We realize that this is not the common opinion of the men of the world today, but certainly every believer ought to recognize the fact that second only to conversion, more is involved in marriage than any other decision which a Christian is called upon to make. Make it seriously, carefully, and prayerfully, and then expect the blessing of the Lord.

*Chapter Fourteen*

## CHRISTIAN LIBERTY

> Now as touching things offered unto idols, we know that we all have knowledge. Knowledge puffeth up, but charity edifieth.
> And if any man think that he knoweth any thing, he knoweth nothing yet as he ought to know.
> But if any man love God, the same is known of him (I Corinthians 8:1-3).

HAVING disposed of the perplexing problem of marriage in I Corinthians 7, Paul now takes up another burning question in Corinth:

> Now as touching things offered unto idols (I Corinthians 8:1a).

This is a brand new subject, but only one of the many problems in this carnal church. The Corinthians were a congregation of immature Christians who were still in their childhood as far as Christian experience was concerned. And they had more problems and difficulties and questions than there are hairs upon one's head. Proud, haughty, self-sufficient, and boasting of their superior knowledge and spirituality, they knew not that they were carnal, and acted like a group of children. They were arguing and fighting and bickering over non-essentials and splitting hairs over personal liberties and private interpretations.

### CONCERNING MEATS

In a letter written to Paul the Corinthians had mentioned a great many of these problems on which they sought his help and advice. They needed light on the matters of dealing with an immoral member, mixed marriages and divorce. And now

Paul takes up the next problem, a brand new problem, that of Christian liberty under grace.

The question of buying and eating legally unclean foods, foods bought in a heathen temple, had come up, and had become a subject of a serious controversy among the members of the church. The majority of the believers in Corinth seemed to be liberal in their views and held that it was perfectly right and proper to eat meats which had been previously presented as an offering and sacrifice in a pagan temple. There were others, however, who considered it wicked and absolutely wrong, and the result was two separate factions, each one of them condemning the other.

## Jew and Gentile

Probably the fact that the church contained both converted Jews and Gentiles was the source of controversy. The distinction between the clean and the unclean animals had been for centuries an insuperable barrier to fellowship between Jew and Gentile. Wherever the devout Jew lived he required a special butcher to prepare his meat, one who was trained to decide whether the meat was killed according to the law or not. The Jew would under no circumstances eat meat which had not been certified as free from legal blemish and officially prepared according to the law. The custom today still prevails in the eating of specially prepared "kosher" meat. But the Gentiles had been accustomed to obtain their meat anywhere, as long as it was good to eat, and they made no distinction between clean and unclean animals. Much of this meat which was sold in these pagan temples consisted of remnants of sacrifices brought to the heathen altars and placed on sale after the priests had used their own portion for ceremonial purposes and their own private use. It was meat of the very highest quality, for nothing but the best was accepted by the priests in sacrifice to their heathen gods. Moreover, it was usually cheap, for it was donated for sacrifice, and therefore it was a boon to poor Christians who might not otherwise enjoy this highest quality meat.

The legalists said, however, that it was wrong to eat such meat because it had been offered unto idols and served in an ungodly heathen temple; while those who took a more liberal view contended that there was nothing wrong with it because they were under grace. And so the controversy waxed hotter, and hotter, until they were compelled to turn to Paul for his solution of the question. And now notice Paul's answer.

## PAUL'S ANSWER

As concerning therefore the eating of those things that are offered in sacrifice unto idols, we know that an idol is nothing in the world, and that there is none other God but one.

For though there be that are called gods, whether in heaven or in earth, (as there be gods many, and lords many,)

But to us there is but one God, the Father, of whom are all things, and we in him; and one Lord Jesus Christ, by whom are all things, and we by him (I Corinthians 8:4-6).

Paul's answer is direct and to the point. He says that the meat offered to idols is just as good as any other meat which might have been purchased elsewhere. We are not under the law, but under grace. By eating, therefore, in an idol's temple, Paul asserts, I am not endorsing the idol or the temple or the practice of the pagan priests. I completely ignore them. I would not even recognize their existence by refraining from going there and eating in their idol temple. The fact that the meat was offered to idols or is served or sold in a pagan temple does not affect the meat in any sense whatsoever. And to the believer under grace it offers no problem and no objection at all. Paul seems to say, If you want to eat it and have no conscience about the matter, go ahead, there is nothing wrong with eating this meat, even in the ungodly environment of a pagan temple.

## ONLY HALF THE STORY

But now notice carefully that this is only half of the answer which Paul gives. To the enlightened believer under grace there is no problem here at all, for he does not endorse the idol by eating of these controversial meats. But there were others who did not look at it in this light, and did not have the knowledge of grace that some of the others possessed. And these weaker ones considered it an evil thing and their conscience was defiled. These too must be considered and so Paul adds in verse 7:

> Howbeit there is not in every man that knowledge: for some with conscience of the idol unto this hour eat it as a thing offered unto an idol; and their conscience being weak is defiled (I Corinthians 8:7).

There were some who because of early training, background or influence were much offended by the practice of eating these unclean meats, especially partaking of them in an idol's temple. Probably these were the Jewish members in the church of Corinth who found it difficult to forget their legalistic background and the demands of their ceremonial law. Or they may just have been narrow minded souls uninstructed in the liberties of grace. Whoever they were, they considered it wrong and wicked to eat this food and vigorously condemned all who disagreed with them. Paul's answer is:

> But meat commendeth us not to God: for neither, if we eat, are we the better; neither, if we eat not, are we the worse (I Corinthians 8:8).

## NEITHER IS BETTER

Paul says, This is a matter of personal liberty and everyone should be persuaded in his own mind and no one has a right to condemn anyone else for his particular view in the matter. It makes absolutely no difference fundamentally. And so he instructs these Corinthian believers and says, "If you see no harm in it, go ahead, and if you think it wrong, don't do it." It depends upon your own attitude and your background, but let us decide for ourselves and not sit in judgment upon others. The one who eats the meat is not to condemn the one who eats not, nor is the one who abstains from it to judge the one whose conscience permits him to eat it. The evil lies not in either doing it or in not doing it, but in the sin of judging others and of trying to force our personal views upon our fellow believers. Certainly, says Paul, if *you* feel inclined to eat this ceremonially unclean meat, go ahead — *but* only if by so doing you do not offend a weaker brother. It is not only a question of what you have a *right* to do, but what effect your conduct will have on other weaker believers round about you. This is made perfectly clear in verse 9 where Paul says:

> But take heed lest by any means this liberty of yours become a stumblingblock to them that are weak (I Corinthians 8:9).

It is more than a question of personal liberty which should prompt your action, and which enters into your decision. There is also a Christian responsibility involved. There are many things which my conscience, enlightened by grace, permits me to do, but I won't do them because I might offend someone who does not have the same knowledge of grace. Paul therefore uses a direct illustration:

> For if any man see thee which hast knowledge [knowledge of Christian liberty] sit at meat in the idol's temple, shall not the conscience of him which is weak be emboldened to eat those things which are offered to idols;
> And through thy knowledge [of the liberty of grace] shall the weak brother perish, for whom Christ died? (I Corinthians 8:10, 11).

There is therefore nothing wrong in eating in a worldly place such as an idol's temple, but if you are seen by another brother with weak faith and legalistic restraints and tendencies and he should be offended by your liberty or encouraged to do something he feels is wrong, then it becomes a sin for you to do it even though for yourself you have this personal liberty. You cannot claim your liberty then and say, "What I do is nobody else's business." It is your business not to do anything which might cause another believer to be offended or cause him to stumble. If we have the liberty of grace we should be gracious enough to give up our liberty for the sake of a weaker brother. Otherwise your liberty becomes a sin and a stumblingblock, for Paul continues his explanation and says in verses 12 and 13:

> But when ye sin so against the brethren, and wound their weak conscience, ye sin against Christ.
>
> Wherefore, if meat make my brother to offend, I will eat no flesh while the world standeth, lest I make my brother to offend (I Corinthians 8:12, 13).

Personally, therefore, Paul says, I see no harm in going into a pagan temple, even into the temple of the Devil to eat this food, if I can get better meat at a more reasonable cost. But, if in my doing so I become a stumblingblock to another brother, then rather than to offend that brother I will forfeit my liberty and my privilege, and if need be "eat no meat while the earth standeth." This certainly is the acme of graciousness on the part of Paul.

How wonderful it would be if these instructions could be followed by all of us. If all Christians would purpose to walk after this rule, it would solve many problems.

First, we will not judge one another's liberties anymore. If you think that to do something which is not expressly forbidden in the Scriptures is wrong, then refrain from doing it by all means. But do not make the mistake of judging me if my conscience honestly before God permits me this liberty. On the other hand, I am not to do anything which might offend you even though I see absolutely no harm in it for myself.

There are things which I may do which in themselves are not wrong at all for me, but for you it might be a sin, and vice versa. In the matter of harmless amusements, places in which we eat, what we do on certain days, the use of certain foods and of drinks are a personal responsibility. I have no right to judge you or any other believer in these matters, nor have I a right to indulge in them when I know your convictions are the opposite of mine. Grace therefore is to characterize our entire conduct in making the decision on these matters which are not expressly forbidden in the Scriptures.

The question then is never, Have I a right to do this or that, or is this or that in itself a sin? But the question is, Does my conduct glorify God, and does it help or hinder my testimony, and is it a help or a stumblingblock to my weaker brethren? This, then, would at once settle the question of amusements, dress, business practices, and games, and all our Christian privileges. The Lord lays down the rule specifically:

> And whatsoever ye do in word or deed, do all in the name of the Lord Jesus (Colossians 3:17).

That is the test by which we are to evaluate everything which is of a questionable nature. It is not a matter of legality, but a matter of honestly facing the question, Is this thing which we are doing to the glory of God, and is it a help or hindrance to those round about us?

> Let us not therefore judge one another any more: but judge this rather, that no man put a stumblingblock or an occasion to fall in his brother's way (Romans 14:13).

## Chapter Fifteen

# LIVING BY GRACE

> All things are lawful for me, but all things are not expedient: all things are lawful for me, but all things edify not (I Corinthians 10:23).

THE believer in Christ is not under the law, but under grace (Romans 6:14). The believer is dead to the law (Galatians 2:19). The believer is free from the law (Romans 7:4). He is delivered from the law (Romans 7:16). And in Romans 10:4, we read:

> For Christ is the end of the law for righteousness to every one that believeth (Romans 10:4).

If there was any one single thing which Paul was dead set against, it was against being put back under the law from which he had been delivered by the grace of God. For many years Paul had lived under the law of Moses, and done his very utmost extended best to keep that law in all sincerity, so that he could say, "as touching the law, blameless"; and yet at the end of all those years of struggling to keep the law he found himself a poor lost sinner standing in the need of the mercy and grace of God. Paul knew the utter futility of trying to please God by his own works, and therefore, was ready to fight to the finish those who would bring him back under the bondage of the law.

And so Paul repeats *four times* in this one epistle to the Corinthians the statement, "All things are lawful for me." As far as the law is concerned, I am free. Now, don't misunderstand that statement, for Paul did not say that he could do anything he pleased, and there would be no wrong in it.

Ah, no, quite to the contrary. What Paul says is this: As far as the "law of Moses" goes, I am not under it any longer. But I am now under the law of grace, and my Christian conduct is now motivated by a higher law, the law of love for God and a gracious consideration of my fellow brethren, even those who may disagree with me. Our service under grace is just as punctual as the law ever demanded, and more so, but it is not merely because the law commands it. It is not legal, but the result of gratitude for His great deliverance. The true believer will seek to do God's will and follow His commandments to be sure, but not only because the law demands it, but because grace expects it. Personally, the believer is not under the law in any sense, but stands in the perfect liberty of grace. *But* as a member of the body of Christ and of society, his conduct is determined by another rule, and that is, the glory of God and his influence and effect upon other people. Paul had been setting forth this great truth in I Corinthians 8 which we have studied, and also referred to in Romans 14. To show how necessary it is to get the importance of this fact of our liberty in grace, he uses an illustration in verse 27:

> If any of them that believe not bid you to a feast, and ye be disposed to go; whatsoever is set before you, eat, asking no question for conscience sake (I Corinthian 10:27).

Here indeed is the problem. Suppose that an unbeliever, an unsaved person, should ask you as his guest to a feast in his home, or probably in an idol's temple if you lived in Paul's day. What would you do? Remember the invitation comes from an unbeliever, an unsaved infidel. If you have conscientious scruples about it, because at an unbeliever's feast ceremonially and legally unclean food would be served, then you should not go. Remember, this is in Corinth, a heathen city, given over to idolatry. But, says Paul, if you want to go, there is no harm in going. As Paul puts it, "If ye be disposed to go" then go ahead, eat what they serve and enjoy yourself, asking no questions.

### THE INEVITABLE "BUT" AGAIN

But there is one condition attached to this liberty. Listen to it in verse 28:

> But if any man say unto you, This [meat] is offered in sacrifice unto idols, eat not for his sake that shewed it, and for conscience sake: for the earth is the Lord's and the fulness thereof:
>
> Conscience, I say, not thine own, but of the other: for why is my liberty judged of another man's conscience?
>
> For if I by grace be a partaker, why am I evil spoken of for that for which I give thanks?
>
> Whether therefore ye eat, or drink, or whatsoever ye do, do all to the glory of God (I Corinthians 10:28-31).

You see the point, I trust. If that which you do under grace, in the liberty of faith, offends someone else, then it becomes sin, if you, knowing you are offending a brother, continue in it. You may reply, as Paul states it here, "Why is my liberty judged of another man's conscience? Why am I evil spoken of for that for which I give thanks?" Why should I deny myself this pleasure just because some narrow-minded legalist finds fault with it. And the answer is this, "No man liveth unto himself." The question is not *my liberty* and *my rights*, but the *glory* of God. People who are saved by grace should be gracious, and since we are saved by grace, we have renounced our own will and seek now only to do the will of God to please Him and our neighbor, and not ourselves. That, my friends, is living by grace. That is living unto God, and that is what Paul means when he says:

> For I through the law am dead to the law, that I might live unto God (Galatians 2:19).

The question is not one of legality at all, but, What can I do to please Him who hath redeemed me by His grace? I serve Him, not because I fear punishment if I don't obey, or I lose my salvation, but I serve Him because He has so wonderfully saved me and given me eternal life.

### SOME PRACTICAL CONSIDERATIONS

People who talk about grace should be gracious. It is a sad, sad thing that many, many believers including fundamentalists, who are always talking about grace, grace, grace, are often the most legal Christians in all the world. They lay down rules and laws, and judge one another, and find fault, and condemn and exclude. If you don't part your hair like they do, conform to all their local and often provincial "do's" and "don'ts" and customs, you are excluded from their fellowship. If you are born again, my friend, and washed in the blood, you are my brother in Christ, and I want fellowship with you. I may not agree with you in all things, but let's disagree in love, and let us at least be gracious about our differences, and seek to help one another.

Let us not judge one another any more, but seek to help and instruct and correct in the spirit of love and graciousness. Are you prone to judge and criticize others for things they do, about which they may have no scruples at all? Ninety-nine times out of a hundred, when we judge some sin in others, we are only throwing up a smoke screen to divert attention away from some sin or habit in our own lives which may even be ten times worse than the one which we condemn in the life of someone else. I do not find one verse in the Bible which tells me to judge my neighbor, but rather that we are to judge ourselves. We may judge sin and error in people's lives, but we are never to judge one another. And when we start looking into our own hearts and lives, we find so many faults, that others will look like angels in comparison. You are very censorious and critical about something your brother does, but do you realize that you are judging him, which may be an even greater sin? Do you ever judge the politer but more serious sins of your own life? Do you ever gossip? Do you ever whisper? Ever pass along to others some sin or fault of a friend? Listen! The Bible has far more to say about gossip than the fault which you are so mercilessly condemning in your brother at this very time. Gossip is worse than stealing a man's possessions. These may be replaced, but a good name stolen through careless gossip can never be replaced. Slander is more than merely spreading derogatory things about a neighbor. It is murder, murdering a man's reputation, never to be undone. Before you judge your brother again for something your self-righteous soul condemns, ask yourself the question, Am I guilty of some of the things the Bible condemns in me, while it is probably utterly silent concerning that thing I am so scathingly denouncing in my neighbor? You can condemn your neighbor for being a spendthrift, but are you covetous? I know people who would condemn a poor man for filching a loaf of bread because his family was starving, and yet, while the self-righteous accuser of this poor man loudly howls for the indictment of the poor fellow for petty larceny, he himself is as covetous as the Devil himself, and has never known what it is to see his children hungry and cold.

There is a worse sin than a poor man stealing a loaf of bread. We do not justify the theft, but it may be just as great a sin to sit in judgment upon him, when you have an abundance and don't know what poverty or hunger is. Are you stingy? Have you an unforgiving spirit? Are you proud? Ah, friends, these are the politer sins which do not come up for condemnation, but according to the Word of God they are denounced even more vigorously than many a fault which you may condemn in your fellow man.

## Are You Gracious?

People who have been saved by the grace of God should always be gracious. Do you think of others rather than only of yourself? You see, this enters into every single department of our lives. It is the little things which are the evidence of grace in our everyday life. You see, I am trying to get this thing of grace down to where you and I live. That's what is wrong with the world today. Everything runs by law, instead of by love. We stand on our legal rights instead of acting in grace toward one another. Ah, my friends, if you were to receive your just deserts and your rights, you would be lost today, but by His grace you have been saved. Let us listen to the words of grace as found in Ephesians 4: 29-32:

> Let no corrupt communication proceed out of your mouth, but that which is good to the use of edifying, that it may minister grace unto the hearers.
> And grieve not the holy Spirit of God, whereby ye are sealed unto the day of redemption.
> Let all bitterness, and wrath, and anger, and clamour, and evil speaking, be put away from you, with all malice:
> And be ye kind one to another, tenderhearted, forgiving one another, even as God for Christ's sake hath forgiven you.

There is a pattern of grace, (not law, but grace) — forgiving because we have been forgiven.

Now I have tried to be very direct and plain in speaking to you, and I do hope and pray that you will also be gracious in receiving this message. Maybe you do not agree with all I have said, especially concerning our freedom from the law. Maybe you differ sharply with some things which I have said, but if you do, be gracious about it. Some of you have written to me, in a very condemnatory tone, consigning me to judgment itself, because I have preached grace, and grace alone, wholly apart from human merit. Some of you have accused me of preaching "that damnable doctrine of free grace." Now, beloved, that is not gracious. Of course, if you are under the law, then that explains your legal and condemnatory attitude, but if you are under grace, you should be gracious. May God help us to put into practice this great principle.

A closing word to the sinner, gathering up what we have said so many times in this series of messages: Your only hope of salvation is to abandon every hope of saving yourself, to give up all your own righteousness and to admit and acknowledge that you have broken every one of God's commandments, that you cannot keep them, that you are under condemnation, and your depraved nature is unable, because of the weakness of the flesh, to please God, and then to cast yourself entirely upon the mercy and the grace of God.

For by grace are ye saved through faith; and that not of yourselves: it is the gift of God:

Not of works, lest any man should boast.

For we are his workmanship, created in Christ Jesus unto good works, which God hath before ordained that we should walk in them (Ephesians 2:8-10).

And just one closing word to those of you who are believers. Jesus has set us an example. We read,

For even Christ pleased not himself (Romans 15:3a).

And again,

I come to do thy will, O God (Hebrews 10:9a).

We then that are strong ought to bear the infirmities of the weak, and not to please ourselves.

Let every one of us please his neighbour for his good to edification (Romans 15:1-2).

*Chapter Sixteen*

## THE LIBERTY OF GRACE

> Who goeth a warfare any time at his own charges? who
> planteth a vineyard, and eateth not of the fruit thereof? or
> who feedeth a flock, and eateth not of the milk of the flock?
> (I Corinthians 9:7).

PAUL was unmarried and often traveled alone. Oftentimes he
needed a woman secretary, but refrained from having one to
travel with him, because he would give no occasion for offense
or criticism among the believers. He had a perfect legal
right, because of his physical condition, but grace caused him
to forebear. In the same way Paul also refused to accept a
salary or remuneration for his services at Corinth for a whole
year and a half. Instead of taking a single penny, he worked
with his own hands to make a living, and to keep body and
soul together. Now all of this was entirely voluntary. Paul
did not have to do this, nor was he compelled to do so because of any commandment in the Word. "The laborer is
worthy of his hire," and "they that preach the gospel shall
live by the gospel." All of this, however, illustrates the liberty
of grace. Grace causes us to go way beyond the demands of
the law, and to sacrifice our legal rights. Paul had a perfect
right to expect these Corinthians to whom he ministered in
spiritual things to support him in physical things, and if he had
a wife, to support her as well. He had a perfect right to
expect this, but he gave it all up for the sake of stopping all
criticism and giving no offense in any way, and to eliminate
any accusation of commercializing the Gospel. Paul would
have no one accuse him of preaching for the money that was

in it. No one was going to accuse Paul of running a gospel racket by his high-powered methods, his emphasis upon offerings, by schemes to get people to give, by high-pressure appeals for money, by gadgets and tricks, gimmicks and hard-luck stories, and begging tactics to separate the Corinthians from their possessions. But even though Paul abhorred all of these unscriptural methods, he insists he has a right to expect those to whom he preached to support him comfortably. Listen to his argument:

> Who goeth a warfare any time at his own charges (I Corinthians 9:7a).

The soldier expects to be, and he should be adequately paid.

> Or who planteth a vineyard, and eateth not of the fruit thereof? (I Corinthians 9:7b).

Certainly the laborer is worthy of his hire, and Paul seems to say, "I have a right to look to you for support, since I am ministering to you of the spiritual things which the Lord has committed to my trust." But now notice carefully the verses which follow:

> Say I these things as a man? or saith not the law the same also?
>
> For it is written in the law of Moses, Thou shalt not muzzle the mouth of the ox that treadeth out the corn. Doth God take care [make provision] for oxen?
>
> Or saith he it altogether for our sakes? For our sakes, no doubt, this is written: that he that ploweth should plow in hope; and that he that thresheth in hope should be partaker of his hope (I Corinthians 9:8-10).

Paul reminds these Corinthian Christians that even the law makes provision for the worker. If this be true under the law, how much more is this true under grace? If this be true of material things, how much more of spiritual things? And so he continues in verse 11,

> If we have sown unto you spiritual things, is it a great thing if we shall reap your carnal things? (things for the body) (I Corinthians 9:11).

Yes, says Paul, I have a right to expect your full and willing financial support. Those who give their full time to the

Gospel have a right to live of the Gospel. However, Paul was willing to forego all of this, and give up his lawful rights in order that he might not in any way give occasion to others to find fault with his ministry. Of course, we realize that there are those who see in Paul's conduct an argument against a paid ministry, but they miss the point entirely. Paul did not refuse a salary, or material remuneration because it was wrong, or because he had no right to it, but because he wanted to stop the mouths of these fault-finders once and for all, who would say that Paul was preaching for the financial gain which he was able to get. And so Paul continues:

> If others [the other apostles, preachers, evangelists, and missionaries] be partakers of this power over you, are not we rather? (I Corinthians 9:12).

Others, says Paul, were supported by you; and of course, it was perfectly proper that they should be; but, says Paul:

> Nevertheless we have not used this power; but suffer all things, lest we should hinder the gospel of Christ.
>
> Do ye not know that they which minister about holy things live of the things of the temple? and they which wait at the altar are partakers with the altar?
>
> Even so hath the Lord ordained that they which preach the gospel should live of the gospel.
>
> But I have used none of these things: neither have I written these things, that it should be so done unto me: [I am not begging] for it were better for me to die, than that any man should make my glorying void.
>
> For though I preach the gospel, I have nothing to glory of: for necessity is laid upon me; yea, woe is unto me, if I preach not the gospel (I Corinthians 9:12-17).

The ministry of preaching was not just a job with the apostle Paul. It was not another way of just making a living, just a profession, but it was a divine call, an imperative call, an inescapable responsibility. Paul was not a preacher by choice. He was a preacher by conviction. He was not just in it to make an easy living. No, says Paul:

> Woe is unto me, if I preach not the gospel (I Corinthians 9:16b).

## A Far Cry

It is a far cry from that testimony of Paul to the all too prevalent idea of the gospel ministry today. Paul dignified and adorned the ministry, not by putting on pious airs, but by a godly life and a holy example before others. He suffered poverty and want, and privation, not because he had to, but to remove all suspicion and occasion for criticism.

Oh, that we might learn the lesson of the apostle Paul. We fully agree that it is perfectly right and proper that preachers and Christian workers should be supported, so that they can give their entire time to their ministry without spending half of their time keeping the wolves from the door. I believe that the faithful minister of the Gospel should be relieved of as much of the cares for material things as possible, so that he may give himself entirely to the ministry of the Word of God. A preacher has a right to live as well and as comfortable as his flock. The priest in the Old Testament had only one job, and that was to serve in the temple and at the altar. And then all of his needs were freely supplied by those to whom he ministered. But in too many instances this provision has been grossly abused and exploited.

One of the most frequent criticisms which we hear today is that the ministry has become a racket. All ministers are after, we are told, is the dollar. In too many of our gospel meetings, a good proportion of the time is taken up in taking the offering with high-pressured build-ups, clever jokes, hard-luck stories, and other devious and dubious means of extracting money from reluctant and unwilling donors. We have listened to evangelists and Bible teachers tell their tales of woe, how they gave up or turned down a business career, or an acting career, or gave up the stage at $2,000.00 a week, or left a lucrative practice of law or medicine, to become poor, impoverished preachers of the Gospel. Oh, beloved, let us cease talking about making sacrifices, and talk of His sacrifice. When I was called from a successful practice of medicine to the gospel ministry, it was NOT a sacrifice — it was a promotion for me. I have never regretted it.

How often we have wished that the preaching of the Gospel could be carried on without ever mentioning money or material needs. Some programs are little less than a build-up for the offering which is to follow. It seems that everybody has some pet project. Many people tell us that they are even afraid to write for our literature lest they get their names on another sucker list for life, to be regularly and systematically bombarded by high-powered promotion material with its beg for more, more and more money. If God's people are properly taught to know the grace of God, all of these methods become unnecessary and the work of Christ will never suffer.

## Back To Paul

But we must get back to Paul before we close this chapter:

> For if I do this thing willingly, I have a reward: but if against my will, a dispensation of the gospel is committed unto me (I Corinthians 9:17).

Willingly or unwillingly, says Paul, I *must* preach the Gospel. And if I do it gladly without any thought of present reward, then I shall receive my reward worth while by and by. Listen to Paul's words:

> What is my reward then? Verily that, when I preach the gospel, I may make the gospel of Christ without charge, that I abuse not my power (my privilege to receive support) in the gospel (I Corinthians 9:18).

## Judgment Seat of Christ

Paul was able to do all this because he looked beyond the present needs. He had his eye on the rewards, at the Judgment Seat of Christ, at the coming of the Lord. And this is the force of the balance of the chapter.

> For though I be free from all men, yet have I made myself servant unto all, that I might gain the more.
>
> And unto the Jews I became as a Jew, that I might gain the Jews; to them that are under the law, as under the law, that I might gain them that are under the law;

> To them that are without law, as without law, (being not
> without law to God, but under the law to Christ,) that I
> might gain them that are without law.
> To the weak became I as weak, that I might gain the weak:
> I am made all things to all men, that I might by all means
> save some.
> And this I do for the gospel's sake, that I might be partaker
> thereof with you (I Corinthians 9:19-23).

The burning desire, the impelling motive, the almost
fanatical desire to please only God, influenced and prompted
Paul's entire action in his ministry. He was not concerned
with success, but he was vitally concerned with faithfulness.
And so he concludes the chapter by giving his reason for his
gracious action in all of these matters. He has his eye on the
Judgment Seat of Christ, when the Lord is going to reward.

There is going to be a special reward and crown for those
who faithfully minister the Word to God's people. The Bible
is very explicit on this matter. Listen to the inspired words of
the apostle Peter:

> The elders which are among you I exhort, who am also
> an elder, and a witness of the sufferings of Christ, and also
> a partaker of the glory that shall be revealed:
> Feed the flock [not, shear the flock] of God which is among
> you, taking the oversight thereof, not by constraint . . . not
> for filthy lucre, but of a ready mind;
> Neither as being lords over God's heritage, but being en-
> samples to the flock.
> And when the chief Shepherd shall appear, ye shall receive
> a crown of glory that fadeth not away (I Peter 5:1-4).

Those who faithfully serve as pastors, teachers, evangelists,
and Christian workers may expect like Peter to be partakers
of the sufferings of Christ, but also of the glory that shall be
revealed.

I know the price we have to pay for faithfulness. Sometimes it may seem hard and difficult. My heart goes out to
God's faithful preachers, pastors, and evangelists in the hard
and difficult places. I pray constantly for you that you may
keep your eye on the glory, that when the chief Shepherd

shall appear ye also may receive a crown of glory that fadeth not away. The moment we meet Jesus our troubles will be forgotten, and we shall look back and feel ashamed that we have ever murmured or complained here below.

> Oft times the days seem drear,
> Our trials hard to bear,
> We're tempted to complain,
> To murmur and despair.
> But Christ will soon appear,
> To catch His Bride away,
> All sorrow will be ended,
> In God's eternal day.
>
> It will be worth it all,
> When we see Jesus.
> Life's trials seem so small,
> When we see Christ.
> One glimpse of His dear face,
> All sorrow will erase.
> Then bravely run the race,
> Till we see Christ.
>
> —*Esther Kerr Rusthoi*

*Chapter Seventeen*

# EGYPT AND CANAAN

Moreover, brethren, I would not that ye should be ignorant, how that all our fathers were under the cloud, and all passed through the sea;

And were all baptized unto Moses in the cloud and in the sea;

And did all eat the same spiritual meat;

And did all drink the same spiritual drink: for they drank of that spiritual Rock that followed them: and that Rock was Christ.

But with many of them God was not well pleased: for they were overthrown in the wilderness.

Now these things were our examples, to the intent we should not lust after evil things, as they also lusted (I Corinthians 10:1-6).

Now all these things happened unto them for ensamples: and they are written for our admonition, upon whom the ends of the world are come (I Corinthians 10:11).

IN Paul's plea for godliness and service among believers, he turns for an illustration to the history of the nation of Israel. And all these things were written for our example and for our instruction. Israel as a nation constituted God's people in the Old Testament. The Israelites were held in Egyptian bondage. By one man, Moses, they were delivered from Egypt by the blood of the lamb, passed through the Red Sea and started their journey to Canaan.

This is according to Paul a typical picture of the church at Corinth. Egypt represents the world, wherein they were under judgment and bondage. But through one man, the Lord Jesus Christ, of whom Moses was only the type, they had been

113

delivered by the blood of the lamb. By God's judgment of the Devil (represented by Pharaoh and his armies) they were forever separated from the Egypt of their condemnation. In all of this the history of Israel is typical of the experience of the salvation of all believers everywhere since.

### MANNA AND WATER

However, after the Israelites had been delivered from Egypt, God does not abandon them to find their way to the Promised Land, but He also made provision for their sustenance and keeping on the way. He gave them a cloud to guide them, by day and by night. He gave them manna from heaven and water from the rock until they reached the land of victory in Canaan. All of this is typical of the life of believers. God has not only made provision to save us, but also made full provision to keep us, after we have been saved. He gave the Holy Spirit to guide us, the manna of the presence of Christ to feed us, and the water of the Word to sanctify us. In all the history of Israel we see a shadow, a figure, a type of believers in this dispensation. This is the force of the words of the apostle Paul:

> Now all these things happened unto them for ensamples: and they are written for our admonition (I Corinthians 10:11).

The nation of Israel, however, though a redeemed people, fell short of the perfect standard which God had placed before them. In this, too, they are typical of all believers. This does not mean that every Israelite was saved. Paul is not speaking of any individual Israelite, but the nation Israel, and the nation was a redeemed people who represented the Church of the living God. They therefore point to the redeemed believers, for he opens this passage with: "Moreover brethren."

He is addressing brethren and believers in the Lord Jesus Christ. But even though all the nation of Israel were delivered from Egypt under the blood, and forever separated from the land of Egypt and its judgment, they did not all reach Canaan. Paul says:

But with many of them God was not well pleased: for they were overthrown in the wilderness (I Corinthians 10:5).

Superficial reading of this passage might lead one to believe that those who were once saved could be ultimately lost. Viewing this thing only on the surface, one might come to this conclusion. But this would be doing violence to Paul's intention. A great number of the nation of Israel certainly never reached the land of Canaan, but their carcasses fell in the wilderness, *not in Egypt*. They were still *out* of Egypt. They were still under the blood. Out of Egypt, but they fell short of Canaan. They represent those believers who are saved and redeemed by the blood of Christ, but who, like the carnal Corinthian believers, never reach the place of victory. They are *out* of the place of judgment of the world, but *not* in the place of victory and full service for the Lord. They fall short of God's best. All of the people of Israel twenty years and over who left Egypt fell in the wilderness with the exception of only two men, Joshua and Caleb.

## CANAAN NOT HEAVEN

Of the millions who are saved there are only a few who ever reach the land of victory, who ever know the joy of living above the circumstances of life. They are still saved, but come short of God's best for them. Now all this becomes clear when we remember that Canaan in the Bible does not represent heaven. The Jordan river does not represent death. It is rather a picture of leaving behind the wilderness of Christian defeat and doubts and failures, and experiencing daily victory over our enemies, the world, the flesh, and the Devil. Canaan is typical of VICTORY in the Christian life. It is not a picture of heaven. In Canaan, the Israelites still had their enemies to subdue. They still had wars to fight, and had to face many a battle to possess the land. Certainly in heaven we shall have no battles or struggles, or enemies to meet. Canaan then is *not* heaven, but speaks of victory here.

### SOLEMN WARNING

Only a few of the nation of Israel ever reached this land of victory. Redeemed Israel does not, we repeat, mean that every individual Israelite was saved. The redeemed Israelites are only typical of the redeemed of this dispensation. They were redeemed from physical bondage. Every one under the blood was delivered from the bondage of Egypt, *never* to return again. And so they become a picture of our spiritual deliverance. If we are saved, we are out of the Egypt of condemnation, and the sin question is settled for us forever. But we still may come short of the best that God has and may fail to reach the land of victory.

How fitting this admonition to the Corinthian believers. They were saved, but defeated. They were troubled with carnality and selfishness, unjudged sin and all sorts of doctrinal and moral error. And Paul reminds them of what happened to the Israelites. They died in the wilderness. How many Christians die in the wilderness. They never come to the place of full surrender, complete consecration, and complete joy, and complete fruitbearing for the Lord Jesus. They lack assurance, constantly doubt, and are devoid of the joy and the victory which is possible for all those who are willing to be obedient to the will of God.

This sin, God is going to judge. He may judge it now by sending chastening, sickness, and weakness. He may even take the believer home to heaven to be judged at the Judgment Seat of Christ. Paul explains this fully in I Corinthians 11, and we will take up this matter when we consider that chapter.

And so Paul concludes with this solemn admonition:

> Neither be ye idolaters, as were some of them; as it is written, The people sat down to eat and drink, and rose up to play.
>
> Neither let us commit fornication, as some of them committed, and fell in one day three and twenty thousand.
>
> Neither let us tempt Christ, as some of them also tempted, and were destroyed of serpents.
>
> Neither murmur ye, as some of them also murmured, and were destroyed of the destroyer.

Now all these things happened unto them for ensamples: and they are written for our admonition, upon whom the ends of the world are come.

Wherefore let him that thinketh he standeth take heed lest he fall (I Corinthians 10:7-12).

It is impossible in the scope of this message to give the full meaning of these words in which Paul warns these Corinthian believers. He mentions a number of things which cause defeat in the life of the Christian. The first of these is idolatry. Now idolatry does not mean that we worship before an idol of stone, or wood, or brass, or any material object. Idolatry may be any thing which we place before the Lord. It may consist of our own will, it may consist of our pride or some unconfessed sin. It may consist of covetousness. We may make idols of many things in our lives, and these are hindrances which prevent us from knowing the fullness of the joy and the victory in the Lord Jesus Christ. The second thing which Paul mentions is pleasure. The people sat down to eat and to drink and rose up to play. This, too, can become an obstacle when we live for material things, and do not heed the admonition of our Lord who said:

But seek ye first the kingdom of God, and his righteousness; and all these things shall be added unto you (Matthew 6:33).

Then he mentions the grosser sins, the sin of fornication as some of the Israelites committed and fell in one day three and twenty thousand. This sin of fornication was judged by the Lord by death, as we have seen in a previous chapter where a man who continued in uncleanness and licentiousness was delivered unto Satan for the destruction of the flesh that the spirit might be saved in the day of Jesus Christ. The next thing Paul mentions in this chapter is "tempting Christ." Numbers 21 relates how God sent fiery serpents among the people, which caused the death of great multitudes. The people could only be healed by the raising up of the serpent of brass as a type of the Cross of Calvary. The occasion for their tempting God was that they were dissatisfied with the manna which God had given them from heaven. They complained that it was light food, and they lusted after the food stuffs of the world as represented by the fruits of Egypt. This has a tremendous implication for us when we realize that neglect of the heavenly manna, the Word of God, is tempting the Lord. To ask for more than simply the promises of God is to lay ourselves open to the judgment of God. Another thing Paul mentions is "murmuring." We do not usually consider murmuring or dissatisfaction as sin, and yet it is given in the same connection here with idolatry and fornication and worldliness.

The Lord expects that we shall accept from His hand that which He feels is best for us, without murmuring, and without questioning, and without repining. This is the life of victory and leads us finally to Canaan. Remember that all these things were done unto the Israelites for our examples. And we should profit by them.

We certainly have had ample warning of how God deals with these sins in the history of Israel, and we are thereby warned that continuing in unconfessed sin will call for the judgment of God, either here or at the Judgment Seat of Christ. But God has not only clearly revealed His judgment upon the sins of the believer, but He has also provided a remedy. How graciously therefore this section ends. Here is God's assurance, and I would that we might be able to grasp the full meaning and implication of these divinely and inspired words:

> There hath no temptation taken you but such as is common to man: but God is faithful, who will not suffer you to be tempted above that ye are able; but will with the temptation also make a way to escape, that ye may be able to bear it (I Corinthians 10:13).

And this brings us to the glorious truth of the grace of God, which can enable us to live above the circumstances of life, and not be defeated, but victorious in all that we do. We need not fall short of victory. God wants to forgive us (I John 3:9) and promises us strength for victory.

## Chapter Eighteen

# WOMEN IN THE CHURCH

SHOULD a Christian woman have her hair bobbed? What is the significance of long hair in the Bible? Is the almost universal custom of bobbing women's hair sanctioned in the Scripture for believers? This delicate question we would like to avoid, if we reasoned according to the flesh; but since the Bible has something to say on the matter, we cannot avoid dealing with it in our series of messages on Corinthians, if we are to declare the whole and complete counsel of God.

We recognize the fact that it will be unpopular with many people, even among believers, but faithfulness to the Word of God prompts us to speak the truth without compromise and leave the judgment with Almighty God. I repeat, we are deeply conscious of the delicacy and the unpopularity of the Biblical position in regard to this matter, and can easily understand the opposition that Paul must have received when he declared himself on this matter. And we suppose that we too will be severely criticized for agreeing with Paul and the Bible, but with Paul we can also say:

> For if I yet pleased men, I should not be the servant of Christ (Galatians 1:10b).

So to the task, for we cannot avoid it. In the opening verses of I Corinthians 11, we find one of the very few passages in this epistle in which Paul commends and praises the church at Corinth. He says:

> Be ye followers of me, even as I also am of Christ.
>
> Now I praise you, brethren, that ye remember me in all things, and keep the ordinances, as I delivered them to you.

In spite of all the evils and the carnality present in this church at Corinth, the members had at least been faithful in keeping the ordinances. They had not kept them faultlessly as we shall see, but they had "kept" them. By the ordinances, of course, he meant "Believers' baptism" and the "Lord's Supper." The word "ordinances" is in the plural (ordinances).

In this chapter Paul is dealing, however, as he did in chapter 10, particularly with the ordinance of the Lord's Supper, and especially the conduct of women at the Lord's Table. It seems from this passage and from chapter 14 that the women had assumed certain privileges and positions and places of authority which were contrary to the revealed Word of God. It seems that women instead of men had taken the lead in the confusion of tongues and had monopolized the meetings with their unwarranted testimonies and prayers. And so Paul puts them in their place and subordinates them to the man in the matters of the assembly.

He is not talking of a woman's place or authority or conduct in the home, but in the assembly, and particularly at the Lord's Table. The setting is the celebration of the ordinance of the Lord's Supper, and here the woman is to assume a place of submission, silence, and respect for her head, the husband. This is not because the woman is inferior in intellect or spirituality, but because of her testimony, and because she is a picture of the bride of Christ in complete subjection to her head. The relation of the Lord Jesus Christ and the Church is symbolized by a husband and a wife. Christ is the Head of the Church, so the husband is the head of the wife; and as the Church is subject to her husband, "so let the wives be to their own husbands in everything." This, of course, implies that the husband is also giving proper respect and love to his wife. And, of course, it is implied and assumed that they are believers as well. This has no application to the unregenerate and the unbeliever. Listen to Paul's argument:

But I would have you know, that the head of every man

is Christ; and the head of the woman is the man; and the head of Christ is God (I Corinthians 11:3).

This is the divine pattern. As Christ became subject and obedient to the Father even unto death, so the believer is to be subject to Christ, his Head, and the wife is to be subject to her head, the husband. Now this subjection is expressed in a peculiar and in a distinctive way. It consists of keeping the head covered, and Paul says in the following verse,

> Every man praying or prophesying, having his head covered, dishonoureth his head.

> But every woman that prayeth or prophesieth with her head uncovered dishonoureth her head [her husband] (I Cor. 11:4, 5).

Now before discussing what this covering consists of, let me point out that this verse does not forbid a woman to testify or pray in the public assembly, as many teach today. It is clearly implied in this passage that the woman is permitted to speak or to pray, but on the one condition that her head be covered when she does so. In the passage in chapter 14, where Paul says, "Let the women keep silence in the churches," he is dealing with "speaking in tongues"; not with conduct at the Lord's Table. He forbids women to speak in tongues in the assembly, at any time, but here in our passage he gives orders on the matter of a head covering while she is speaking or praying. It is therefore definitely implied that if a woman's head is covered, she *is* permitted to speak and to pray, otherwise there would be no point in stating:

> But every woman that prayeth or prophesieth with her head uncovered dishonoureth her head: for that is even all one as if she were shaven (I Corinthians 11:5).

## Hats or Hair

Now for the controversial question. What is meant by "having her head covered"? There are those who claim it refers to a hat or some other little thing which remotely resembles a hat, which must be worn by the women whenever she enters the assembly. Then there are others who say it refers to a woman's hair and that it has nothing to do with artificial coverings. Now it seems that in the light of verse 15 there should be no difficulty. Paul says plainly here,

> But if a woman have long hair, it is a glory to her: for her hair is given her for a covering (I Corinthians 11:15).

The covering which Paul speaks of in this verse is "long hair," in its primary implication. It is called her "glory." It is the badge of her obedience and submission to her own husband. It is a sign of dignified femininity, and so to have it bobbed constitutes a denial of the authority of her husband, and a sign of insubjection to her head. It destroys the beautiful type of the subjection of the Church to her Lord. And then Paul gives his argument:

> For if the woman be not covered, let her also be shorn: but if it be a shame for a woman to be shorn or shaven, let her be covered.
>
> For a man indeed ought not to cover his head, forasmuch as he is the image and glory of God: but the woman is the glory of the man.
>
> For the man is not of the woman; but the woman of the man.
>
> Neither was the man created for the woman; but the woman for the man.
>
> For this cause ought the woman to have power on her head because of the angels.
>
> Nevertheless neither is the man without the woman, neither the woman without the man, in the Lord.
>
> For as the woman is of the man, even so is the man also by the woman; but all things of God.
>
> Judge in yourselves: is it comely that a woman pray unto God uncovered?
>
> Doth not even nature itself teach you, that, if a man have long hair, it is a shame unto him?
>
> But if a woman have long hair, it is a glory to her: for her hair is given her for a covering (I Corinthians 11:6-15).

We refrain from general comment since it is evident and clear that the primary meaning of the word "covering" here refers to the hair. However, one statement challenges our attention, and it is found in verse 10, which gives one reason for the covering of the head in the assembly.

> For this cause ought the woman to have power on her head because of the angels (I Corinthians 11:10).

We believe that holy angels who worship and adore the Lord are present when the saints remember the Lord, and because of their ministering presence everything should be according to God's will. We know that the angels are called "ministering" servants, to minister unto them that shall be the heirs of salvation, and we have every reason to believe that they are present as the servants of God to minister to our needs and especially when we come together to remember the Lord's death. We, therefore, believe that the custom of Christian women wearing short hair is contrary to the Scriptures and against the clear teaching of the Word of God. Ponder carefully the words once more:

> If a woman have long hair, it is a glory to her: for her hair is given her for a covering (I Corinthians 11:15).

Now I realize that many of you will disagree, but let us disagree in love. We are stating our opinion as we see it; and without any condemnation of our own, we are only stating the Word of God. If we are wrong in our interpretation and you disagree with us, let us remember that we are still all imperfect. In the meantime, let us be gracious enough to recognize and respect one's private interpretation. I am sure that we will be much safer in being too narrow than in being too broad in regard to some of these controversial issues. Paul seemed also to sense very clearly that this teaching of his would not be universally accepted and would be vigorously opposed, and so he closes this section with verse 16:

> But if any man seem to be contentious, we have no such custom, neither the churches of God (I Corinthians 11:16).

The implication, of course, is that Paul anticipates much opposition and objection to his stand, and dismisses the entire thing and says that if you want to disagree and be contentious, you can be contentious, but this is the revelation of God as I have it and I will stand by it. We'll not argue. If you want to be contentious, it is your concern, not mine.

But there is far more involved here than a mere custom. It is, I believe, a sign of the times. In the Old Testament it was the custom to uncover a woman's head when she had been unfaithful to her husband (Numbers 5:18).

It is, moreover, a significant fact, which cannot be explained as a mere coincidence, that at the same time that bobbing of women's hair came into vogue, women also began the debasing practice of wearing men's apparel.

I say that it is more than mere coincidence that the masculinizing of women's dress and habits has gone hand in hand with the upsurge of immorality, looseness of living and the violation of the marriage vows and the appalling increase in divorce and the resultant evil of broken homes, juvenile delinquency, and all the other evils. Certainly we shall do well to remind you of Romans 12:1, 2:

> I beseech you therefore, brethren, by the mercies of God, that ye present your bodies a living sacrifice, holy, acceptable unto God, which is your reasonable service.
>
> And be not conformed to this world: but be ye transformed by the renewing of your mind, that ye may prove what is that good, and acceptable, and perfect will of God.

"Be not conformed to this world." Dare to be different if need be for Christ. I want to close with the exhortation of the apostle Peter. In speaking to the wives he says:

> Whose adorning let it not be that outward adorning of plaiting the hair, and of wearing of gold, or of putting on of apparel;
>
> But let it be the hidden man of the heart, in that which is not corruptible, even the ornament of a meek and quiet spirit, which is in the sight of God of great price (I Peter 3:3, 4).

*Chapter Nineteen*

## THE LORD'S TABLE

> Now in this that I declare unto you I praise you not, that
> ye come together not for the better, but for the worse.
> For first of all, when ye come together in the church, I hear
> that there be divisions among you; and I partly believe it
> (I Corinthians 11:17, 18).

PAUL opens the eleventh chapter of I Corinthians with a
note of praise for the fact that the Corinthian believers had
kept the ordinances of the Church. However, in our passage
for today, he says, "In this that I declare unto you I praise
you not." Although they kept the ordinances, they did not
keep them in the proper manner, but greatly abused their
privileges when they came together at the Lord's Table. They
apparently had missed the tremendous significance and importance of the ordinance which so vividly commemorates
the death of our Lord Jesus Christ.

Our Lord Jesus before He went to the Cross gathered His
little group of disciples together in the upper room and there
instituted the Lord's Supper, the great feast of the Church
in this dispensation. It is one of the great days in the history
of the Church and the means of a unique and peculiar blessing for the people of God. But like every good thing, the
Devil soon seeks to debauch it and make of it a curse instead
of a blessing. This was true in the early history of the
Church. At the time Paul wrote to the Corinthians the Lord
Jesus had gone back to heaven only about twenty-five years,
and yet in that short period of time evil had crept in to such
an extent that the Lord's Supper had lost almost every ele-

ment of its sacred character. In the church at Corinth had arisen many carnal and fleshly differences. There were divisions among the members, they had grouped themselves in a number of little cliques.

There were at least four of these groups, for Paul tells us in the beginning of the epistle that there were those who said "I am of Paul," "I am of Apollos," "I am of Cephas," and others, "I am of Christ."

This factional and party spirit was carried by these groups even to the Lord's Table. They sat by themselves in little groups as they brake the bread, and cast reproachful and hateful glances across the Table at each other. It seems that one of these parties represented the wealthy folks of the congregation. When the monied people came to the Table of the Lord, they came not only decked in gold and finery but they came with their baskets of expensive food and drink and made a real old-time party of the Lord's Table. Other folks were poor and could not afford these luxuries, and they sat off in a corner with a crust of bread. So far did this evil go that many of them came to the Table of the Lord drunk and debauched. The result was that the Table of the Lord became a scene of strife and debauchery. Notice how Paul describes it:

> Now in this that I declare unto you I praise you not, that ye come together not for the better, but for the worse.
> For first of all, when ye come together in the church, I hear that there be divisions among you; and I partly believe it.
> When ye come together therefore into one place, this is not to eat the Lord's supper.
> For in eating every one taketh before other his own supper: and one is hungry, and another is drunken.
> What? have ye not houses to eat and to drink in? or despise ye the church of God, and shame them that have not? What shall I say to you? shall I praise you in this? I praise you not (I Corinthians 11:17, 18, 20, 21).

Certainly this is an almost unbelievably dark and sad picture, when we remember they were believers. Now to correct these disorders at the Table of the Lord, Paul under inspiration writes the instructions which follow. I realize that this is very familiar ground to most of you but I make no apologies for repeating the truth of this passage often. It needs to be sounded forth again and again and can never be emphasized too much. The sin of coming to the Table of the Lord without proper preparation and a thorough understanding of its meaning is followed by the most serious and terrible results. If Christians would believe, study and conscientiously practice the admonition of this passage it would spare them untold grief and suffering and save them thousands and ten thousands of dollars in time and doctor bills. Hence it is a matter of the very gravest importance. It is ignorance of the will of God which causes much of the sorrow in the life of the believer. Hosea said, "My people are destroyed because of lack of knowledge," and this same thing holds true today. Failure to observe and understand the solemnity and requirements of God's commands and wishes concerning the Lord's Supper are at the bottom of much grief and sickness among the children of God.

We have in this passage from I Corinthians a complete and detailed resume of the meaning and importance of the Lord's Supper. May the Holy Spirit illumine our minds to see His will in our lives and grant us grace to perform it. In studying this passage I would have you notice that Paul gives us SEVEN THINGS CONCERNING THE TABLE OF THE LORD. They are as follows: The Lord's Supper is —

1. A Divine Command.
2. A Blessed Privilege.
3. A Necessary Memorial.
4. A Willing Testimony.
5. A Humbling Confession.
6. An Act of Faith.
7. A Solemn Warning.

Just a word or two about each one but the last.

## A Divine Command

The celebration of the Lord's Supper is a divine command and a solemn obligation which rests upon every one of God's children. Not a child of God lives or ever will live during this age who is not obligated to assemble with the people of God for the celebration of the memorial of the death of Christ in the Lord's Supper. To neglect to do so is to be disobedient to the Lord's direct wish, and the judgment of the Lord will follow upon disobedience. This is very clearly taught us in this passage.

> And when he had given thanks, he brake it, and said, *Take, eat*: this is my body, which is broken for you: *this do* in remembrance of me (I Corinthians 11:24).

There can be no side-stepping the issue. THIS DO. THIS DO. THIS DO. Let it be known therefore that *every Christian is commanded to observe the death of Christ* in the Lord's Supper. If you raise the objection that you are not worthy, then I answer that the only ones who have a right to come to the Table of the Lord are those who *really believe and confess* that they are unworthy. For just such was the Table instituted. If there is sin in your life which prevents you from coming to the Lord's Table, you had better settle that matter immediately and come to the Table, lest God's chastening for your disobedience drive you to the place where you are unwilling to come. THIS DO. THIS DO. Anything which hinders you from coming, must be put away in order that you may come.

## A Blessed Privilege

Moreover we ought to come to the Table and welcome every opportunity to come because of the great privilege the Lord bestows in permitting us to come. The Table of the Lord is the Table *of the Lord*. Think of that. It is not the table of an assembly or a church or a communion or a denomination, but the *Table of the Lord*. Christ is the Host. He is the Master of the house. We poor stumbling faltering creatures, erring every day, unworthy of anything but hell, are invited to come and sit at His, the Lord's Table. We who murdered His Son, we who reviled Him and by our sin spit upon Him and drove the cruel nails through His blessed hands, we are invited to come and sit at His Table with *Him* as our Host and feast with Him by His grace. What a privilege! Do you not see the insult, if any child of God refuses to accept that invitation? O base ingratitude that any of us dare or even let the suggestion arise in our hearts that we will leave our place empty! Surely the Master of the house must deal with you, and will deal with you as a disobedient child if you insult Him by refusing to receive that which He has at infinite cost prepared for you. Remember that the Lord's Table is for *His* people and not for the world. This entire chapter in Corinthians applies only to believers.

## A Necessary Memorial

The Lord's Supper is a necessary memorial given us to remind us at what an infinite cost our salvation has been bought. The Lord said, "THIS DO IN REMEMBRANCE OF ME." What a rebuke! In remembrance of Me! Then God's people may after all forget the great price that was paid for their redemption? Yes, sad, sad though the thought be, it is, alas, all too true. Even we may forget. And *God*, who knows our hearts better than we do, knows that we are yet so human and wayward, that if He did not continually remind us we would soon, so soon, forget. How many times during the week do we forget? And so the Lord tenderly rebukes us in this Supper and says, "You are such unthankful children that if I did not provide a reminder you would all too soon forget what it cost Me to purchase your salvation." And so He has given the Table of the Lord as a reminder, to keep our love aflame and our hearts aglow for Him. He has given it to remind us that we are but dust, and even though we are redeemed we would be unable even to remember Him.

And at the same time the Supper reminds us that it is *His* faithfulness which saves us and not *ours*. If He had forgotten us as we so often forget *Him*, there would be no hope for us at all.

### A WILLING TESTIMONY

But when we come to the Table of the Lord there is still more. In addition to a command, a privilege and a memorial, it is a testimony as well. In verse 26 we read: "For as often as ye eat this bread and drink this cup ye do shew the *Lord's death*." Every time we come together to break bread we are testifying, by the receiving of that bread and cup, that we have experienced in our lives the benefits of the Lord's death and cleansing power of His precious blood. We "declare" the Lord's death. We witness to the fact that we are saved and have appropriated by faith the finished work of the Lord Jesus on our behalf when He died on the cruel cross of Calvary. Every time the child of God, therefore, gathers with the saints about this Table he is witnessing to his personal relationship with Christ. When I take the bread and raise it to my mouth, I testify by that act that I believe that His body was broken for me and His blood was shed for me.

### A HUMBLING CONFESSION

Yet there is more. Not only do we testify in the partaking of the Lord's Supper to our identification with Him in His death but it is a HUMBLING CONFESSION of our own helplessness and unworthiness as well. By my partaking of these elements I confess that my sin was so great, and my iniquity so vile, and my loss so great, that nothing less than the death of the Son of God and the shedding of His precious blood could avail to set me free and wash me clean. Away go all excuses and away go all my own good works. I confess that I was so utterly and hopelessly lost, and my sin was so terrible and so great, that there was nothing in heaven or earth that could pay the price of my sin except the infinite

sacrifice of the most precious One in heaven, namely, the
Lord Jesus Christ. The death of Christ is the death of all
man's righteousness. By this act of celebrating the Supper
of the Lord, I therefore acknowledge myself to be totally
and completely unfit in myself. It means death to pride and
the renouncing of all goodness in myself. I confess as I take
these elements and partake of them that,

> My hope is built on nothing less
> Than Jesus blood and righteousness;
> I would not trust the sweetest frame
> But only lean on Jesus' Name.

And again I confess

> Was it for crimes that I had done,
> He groaned upon the tree?
> Amazing pity, grace unknown,
> And love beyond degree.

### AN ACT OF FAITH

But the Lord's Supper looks not only *backward to the Cross*
but *forward to the Crown* as well. In the verses quoted before, we are told that when we eat the bread and drink the
cup we do show the Lord's death "till *He* come." *Till He
come.* The Lord's Supper is from the *coming* to the *coming.*
It is a memorial that is only for the time of His absence.
When *He comes* we will have no more need for it, for then
we shall *have Him.* The Supper, therefore, looks forward to
His blessed second coming. The reason it will cease then
and we shall drink it new in the Kingdom of Heaven is
simply this, that then we shall be perfect. The Lord's Supper
is an institution for *imperfect people.* It is a command and
privilege for poor failing and stumbling Christians, to strength-
en them and encourage them. Perfect people have no need of
this memorial. So when He comes and we enter perfection,
this Supper will cease and be supplanted by the MARRIAGE
SUPPER OF THE LAMB. You see then the error of many who
believe that no one may come to the Table of the Lord until
they *are good enough.* When a man goes to the Table of

the Lord as a testimony of *his goodness* he is about as unworthy as any one can be. Show me a man who goes to the Lord's Table because he thinks that he is worthy to go and better than others, and I will show you the biggest hypocrite in the assembly. I go to the Lord's Table not to let people know how *good* I am, but on the contrary to acknowledge my *utter unworthiness* and *sinfulness* and to confess that all my hope, and my only hope, lies in *His worthiness,* His death, His sacrifice, for me a poor lost and helpless sinner. Yet in many churches the idea is taught that a man must attain to a certain degree of Christian growth and piety and goodness before he can come. This is the Devil's clever scheme of getting folks who ought to come, to stay away; and getting folks who ought to stay away, to come. This Table is for the poor struggling believers who realize how unworthy they are and who earnestly desire to be forgiven and cleansed and to become more like Jesus. What a humbling confession. In our next message we will take up the solemn responsibility in partaking of the Lord's Supper.

*Chapter Twenty*

## REMEMBERING HIS DEATH

IT is a serious thing to be a Christian. There is far more to being a believer in the Lord Jesus Christ than just making a decision, and then enjoying life and going to heaven when you die. A Christian is expected to be a follower of the Lord Jesus Christ. This is the implied meaning of the word "Christian." It is Christ first. We may break up the word "Christian" as being, "Christ, I Am Nothing," or "Christ Is All Now."

This ownership of Christ every believer confesses when he celebrates the Lord's Supper. In this ordinance, as in no other act of Christian worship, we avow our allegiance to the Lord Jesus Christ, our dependence upon Him. It therefore becomes a terrible thing to partake of the Lord's Table insincerely or indifferently. In our previous message we saw seven great lessons in the Lord's Supper. We pointed out that it is:

1. A Divine Command.
2. A Blessed Privilege.
3. A Necessary Memorial.
4. A Willing Testimony.
5. A Humbling Confession.
6. An Act of Faith.
7. A Solemn Warning.

We come today to the last one of these, the solemn warning, which is implied in the participation in the Lord's Table.

### DIVINE HEALING

The Lord's Supper should never be entered into carelessly, but only after heart-searching self-examination, and confession of every known and doubtful sin. While it is true that we do not come to the Table of the Lord perfectly, we *must come honestly*. Therefore, if any come with known and unconfessed sin in their lives they are inviting certain disaster. If there is in the heart no desire to be really cleansed and separated from sin, and we thus come to the Lord's Table, there are dire judgments promised for such presumptuous sinning. For this reason Paul says:

> Wherefore whosoever shall eat this bread, and drink this cup of the Lord, unworthily, shall be guilty of the body and blood of the Lord (I Corinthians 11:27).

What a serious thing it is. Notice that Paul is speaking to and about *believers*. This does not refer to the unregenerate. Paul is talking about born-again believers who may eat and drink *unworthily*. He is talking about coming to the Table of the Lord with things in life which are not right, and with a deliberate refusal to make them right. For this reason Paul says,

> But let a man examine himself, and so let him eat of that bread, and drink of that cup (I Corinthians 11:28).

We are admonished to examine *ourselves*. Not the other fellow. In many assemblies and churches a great deal of stress is laid upon examining the "other" fellow. But there is nothing of that here. If a man or woman is living a known reproachful life, there are plenty of instructions in the Bible how the church must deal with such; but here we are speaking of *self-examination*. Let a man examine *himself*. He is to make a careful inquest into his own life to see if there be anything that needs to be judged and confessed, leaving not a stone unturned but going right on through. Until he has done this it is a dangerous matter to come to the Lord's Table. And after having examined himself he is not to come until that which was wrong is made right and confessed.

Now what are the consequences to that individual who either will not examine himself, or having examined himself will not go all the way in judging sin in his own life and cleansing it by confession. The Word of God is very clear on this matter.

> For he that eateth and drinketh unworthily, eateth and drinketh damnation to himself, not discerning the LORD's body.
>
> *For this cause* [namely, failure to judge sin in one's own life] *many* [not few] are *weak* and *sickly* among you, and many sleep [are dead].
>
> For if we would judge ourselves, we should not be judged.
>
> But when we are judged, we are chastened of the Lord, that we should not be condemned with the world (I Corinthians 11:29-32).

Solemn words these are. Note a few things in the passage. First, Paul is speaking to Christians. Second, these Christians may eat *judgment to themselves.* The word rendered "damnation" in verse 29 should be "judgment," not damnation. Christians will never be damned, but they will be "judged." Not for the "guilt" of sin but for their walk and works after they are saved.

Then Paul goes on to say what this judgment consists of. Three things are mentioned, namely, SICKNESS, WEAKNESS and DEATH. Because many of the Corinthian Christians had come to the Table of the Lord with unconfessed sin, *many* of them were sick and weak and *many* of them had died. Oh, what a warning and what a responsibility! We are the children of God. He wants us clean. He will have us clean, and if we refuse to take the cleansing of the Word of God through self-examination and confession, the Lord, because He loves us so, takes a hand in the matter *Himself* and cleanses us by His *chastening hand.* It is possible that some cases of sickness among believers are caused by unconfessed sin. For these sicknesses there is little or no earthly remedy. All the money in the world is not enough. There is only one cure for that kind of sickness. It is confession and repentance and self-judgment. However, we hasten here to state that *not all sickness and death is due to sin in the sufferer's life.* We believe the majority of cases of affliction are for other purposes which God has, but we do know that *many* cases of sickness and death are due to the believer's failure to confess sin and to judge sin in his life. Hundreds of dollars are spent annually by Christians for remedies and doctors, with no success.

The remedy lies in *confession* and self-judgment. Notice the next verses:

> For if we would judge ourselves, we should not be judged.
> But when we are judged, we are chastened of the Lord, that we should not be condemned with the world (I Corinthians 11:31, 32).

If we judge the sin in our lives, we shall escape the judgment of God; but if we judge it not, *He will judge* that sin and *chasten* us as His children.

There are today many of God's dear children who are sick and suffering because they refuse to heed this Word concerning self-judgment. What suffering, grief, and expense might be saved and spared if men and women would only take this simple but humbling remedy of the Lord and come in penitent confession.

We believe that the passage in the last chapter of James, so much misconstrued by unscriptural divine healers (so called), applies only to those cases of sickness which are *due to unconfessed and unjudged sin.* The very language indicates this.

> Is any sick among you? let him call for the elders of the church; and let them pray over him, anointing him with oil in the name of the Lord:
> And the prayer of faith shall *save* the sick, and the Lord shall raise him up: and [now note] if he have committed *sins,* they shall be forgiven him (James 5:14, 15).

Now notice how the next verse begins:

> *Confess* your faults one to another, and pray one for another, that *ye may be healed* (James 5:16a).

The whole matter of sickness is here connected with *sins*

and the whole matter of healing has to do with the matter of *confession*.

See then, Christian, what a solemn warning we have here. How imperative that we make this day a day of self-examination. Let every heart be occupied with *judging himself*. See if there be in your life anything that is contrary to His will, and then honestly lay it before Him in confession, and then come to the Table of the Lord.

Now I fear that there are those that will say, "Well, I guess if that is true then I will simply not come to the Table of the Lord. I am not going to lay myself open to the chastening hand of God. I will just not come to the Table at all." Think you to fool God? Think you to get out of it in that way? You shall feel His hand just as severely for that conduct, as for coming without self-judgment. If you do not come because of sin in your life you are *disobedient* and I am warning you that your disobedience *will be* judged. And if you come without confessing your sin, you are equally liable to His chastening. You are in a bad way. If you refuse to come, you are disobedient. If you come but refuse to confess and clean up, you are equally disobedient. There is only one way out. *Examine* yourself, confess to Him. Determine by His grace that you will make right the wrong, and *then come* and receive a blessing. The Christian with sin in his life is in a bad way. There is no way out but through *Him*. And that is why this Table is instituted. For those who feel how far they have come short, how utterly they have failed, who have made a mess of everything, this Table tells them there is cleansing and pardon and forgiveness. Will you take it? Will you avail yourself of it? Will you even now come to Him in true and earnest confession and accept His cleansing? Then come to the Table of the Lord. Come as you are with nothing but the blood as your plea of worthiness.

> Just as I am, without one plea,
> But that Thy blood was shed for me,
> And that Thou bidd'st me come to Thee,
> O Lamb of God, I come, I come.

*Chapter Twenty-one*

## SPIRITUAL GIFTS

> Now concerning spiritual gifts, brethren, I would not have you ignorant (I Corinthians 12:1).

IN the Corinthian church there were many gifts of the Holy Spirit which were given to the believers. These gifts were given to individuals as the Lord willed, and were not necessarily the common experience of all. These gifts were not for each and every believer, but the Lord dispensed them as He saw fit according to His will. Among these gifts were the gifts of teaching or prophesying, the gift of healing, the gift of working miracles, speaking in tongues and the interpretation of these tongues. These were bona fide spiritual gifts present in the Corinthian church and evidences of the Spirit of God in their midst. Paul, however, in this epistle deals specifically with one particular gift, the speaking in tongues. While he makes reference to the other gifts, it is the correction of the evils which accompanied the gift of tongues with which he is particularly occupied because it was the one gift which was being abused more in the Corinthian church than any other. This was the gift which was the least understood and most abused and perverted of all the gifts present in the church. The Corinthian believers were still infants in the faith, immature in Christian experience and were in great need of instruction to correct all the foolish, fanatical, disorderly, childish errors and practices associated with this particular gift which the Lord had bestowed upon them.

Paul wrote, therefore, to correct errors associated with the manifestation of tongues in particular. He did not write primarily to endorse the speaking in tongues, or to forbid it. He wrote to point out the unscriptural use and the counterfeiting of the gift — a result of ignorance of the real purpose of the gift of tongues as bestowed upon the early Church. And so Paul opens this section of three chapters on this subject with these words:

Now concerning spiritual gifts, brethren, I would not have you ignorant (I Corinthians 12:1).

The word "ignorant" gives us the key to these three chapters on this subject. This verse is the key to all that which follows in I Corinthians 12, 13 and 14. He would not have them to be "ignorant" in order that the gift which was given to them for profit, might not be abused and lose its effect and its purpose entirely. That this was the purpose of Paul, to correct their ignorant use of this gift, is evident from the way this section also closes. In I Corinthians 14:38 we read:

But if any man be ignorant, let him be ignorant.

The word "ignorant" therefore is the key to these three chapters on tongues. These Corinthian believers in their ignorance had misinterpreted the place of the gift of tongues entirely, and had pushed it to unscriptural extremes, and the result was disorderliness and abuse and a loss of the blessing which it was intended to convey. Paul says in essence, After I have tried to set you straight in these three chapters, and you still don't understand, then you are just hopeless for correction; and so he concludes the chapters with:

But if any man be ignorant, let him be ignorant (I Corinthians 14:38).

There is nothing further that I can do.

Now before going into the exposition proper of these chapters, we would again like to emphasize the fact that the errors and the extremes in Corinth were the result of ignorance, and the remedy was good, solid, Biblical teaching, the meat of the Word, rather than emotional preaching of the milk of the Word. These Corinthians were converts from paganism and knew little or nothing of the Scriptures. Hence they were in a measure excusable, but not any more after Paul had given them the truth in these three chapters.

Paul reminds them of this in verse 2. He says:

> Ye know that ye were Gentiles, carried away unto these dumb idols, even as ye were led (I Corinthians 12:2).

In the other cities in which Paul had preached, the converts were largely from among the Jews who knew the Old Testament Scriptures, and therefore, were instructed in the Word, and had a good Bible background. But these Corinthian believers were mostly ignorant of the Word of God, and were children and in the need of milk rather than meat. They were still too immature and carnal for solid meat (I Cor. 2:3). In their pagan religion, out of which they had come at their conversion, they were used to all kinds of superstitions, fanaticism, ecstasies, fetishes, and hyper-emotional experiences, and they were not immediately weaned away from these things. They carried much of these over into their Christian life and these remnants of paganism manifested themselves particularly in the abuse of the gift of tongues. Instead of using this God-given gift for its spiritual purpose, they made it the occasion for carnal spiritual pride and self-exaltation and often made it the test of really being saved and having the Holy Spirit.

From verse 3 we infer the awful extremes to which it had led them. Here is the verse:

> Wherefore I give you to understand that no man speaking by the Spirit of God calleth Jesus accursed: and that no man can say that Jesus is the Lord, but by the Holy Ghost.

Some blasphemous and wicked utterances by individuals, under the spurious ecstasy of so-called "tongues," were uttered, as having been inspired by the Spirit of God Himself. The name of Jesus was the most common expression among them. It was Jesus, Jesus, Jesus, while they rejected His Lordship and His authority. They evidently seldom or never used the name, Lord Jesus, but only the name of Jesus.

## MANY GIFTS

The next thing we notice is the purpose of the gifts as given in the Corinthian church. Paul refers to special manifestations of the Spirit in giving to certain individuals these special powers. Men are also called "gifts" in the Scriptures. Every faithful servant of the Lord is "God's gift" to the church to administer the gifts for special service. But all these are by the same Spirit, and therefore, they cannot conflict with one another. And so we read in verses 4 to 7:

> Now there are diversities of gifts, but the same Spirit.
> And there are differences of administrations, but the same Lord.
> And there are diversities of operations, but it is the same God which worketh all in all.
> But the manifestation of the Spirit is given to every man to profit withal (I Corinthians 12:4-7).

From this passage we glean first of all that the gifts of healings, miracles and tongues were genuine spiritual gifts in the early Church. Even though Satan has imitated, copied and counterfeited every one of them, nevertheless, they were originally given by the Spirit of God. They were real and genuine and profitable. While not all had the same gift, they all had the same source and the same purpose and were the gift of the same Spirit. Paul enumerates these gifts:

1. The gift of wisdom. This was for special revelations while the New Testament was still unwritten.
2. The gift of knowledge. This refers to the ability to distinguish error and truth.
3. Works of faith. Ability to resist evil and to live a Godly life.
4. The gift of healing. Referring especially to the healing of the body in those cases where it was the will of the Lord to do so.
5. The gift of miracles. Other signs and wonders different from the gift of healing.
6. The gift of prophecy which here refers mainly to

preaching and teaching these immature Corinthian believers.

7. The discerning of spirits. The ability to distinguish between that which was of the Spirit of God and which was a counterfeit of the Devil.
8. The gift of tongues. And finally,
9. The interpretation of tongues.

### TONGUES PROMINENT

In this epistle, however, Paul deals almost exclusively with the gift of tongues. It had been the most abused and had been given a place of importance way beyond that which the Spirit had intended for it. It was one of the least of the gifts and is mentioned last in the list of the gifts of the Spirit; but the Corinthians had made it first. Their test by which they judged others was, "Do you speak in tongues?", and if not, they implied that you did not have the witness of the Holy Spirit within you. To correct this unscriptural attitude of self-righteousness and carnality, Paul rebukes them.

Notice, therefore, Paul's answer to those who make tongues the test of having the Spirit of God. He says in verses 8 through 11:

> For to one is given by the Spirit the word of wisdom; to another the word of knowledge by the same Spirit;
>
> To another faith by the same Spirit; to another the gifts of healing by the same Spirit;
>
> To another the working of miracles; to another prophecy; to another discerning of spirits; to another divers kinds of tongues; to another the interpretation of tongues:
>
> But all these worketh that one and the selfsame Spirit, dividing to every man severally as he will (I Corinthians 12:8-11).

Seven times the word "another" occurs in these verses. All of the gifts, therefore, or any single gift was not for everyone and anyone, but only for those who were selected by the Spirit of God Himself to receive them. Paul says that the Spirit divides "to every man severally as he himself will."

How utterly false, therefore, to make one's particular experience the inviolable pattern for everyone else's experience, and to condemn those who have had a totally different experience. Paul says that to one is given one gift, and to another, another gift. All the gifts were not present in any one individual, neither did every individual necessarily have to have one single common gift with all other believers. To assert, therefore, that the speaking of tongues is the evidence of the Holy Spirit, is utterly false and unscriptural and the result of ignorance of the Word of God and the purpose for which these gifts were given; and Paul says to such: "Now concerning spiritual gifts, I would not have you ignorant" (I Corinthians 12:1).

### The One Body

Now all this is illustrated by Paul in the figure of the body of Christ. The body consists of many members, all having a different function, but all being essential one to the other:

> For as the body is one, and hath many members, and all the members of that one body, being many, are one body: so also is Christ.
>
> For by one Spirit are we all baptized into one body, whether we be Jews or Gentiles, whether we be bond or free; and have been all made to drink into one Spirit.
>
> For the body is not one member, but many.
>
> If the foot shall say, Because I am not the hand, I am not of the body; is it therefore not of the body?
>
> And if the ear shall say, Because I am not the eye, I am not of the body; is it therefore not of the body?
>
> If the whole body were an eye, where were the hearing? If the whole were hearing, where were the smelling?
>
> But now hath God set the members every one of them in the body, as it hath pleased him.
>
> And if they were all one member, where were the body?
>
> But now are they many members, yet but one body.
>
> And the eye cannot say unto the hand, I have no need of thee: nor again the head to the feet, I have no need of you (I Corinthians 12:12-21).

The point of this passage which we have quoted in full is that we are responsible to God for our own particular gift, and we are to leave the judgment of others entirely in the hands of God. To claim, therefore, that if we do not speak in tongues or have some other gift of the Spirit, we cannot have the witness, is as foreign to the Bible as anything can be. We have a far better and a higher and a more dependable witness of the Spirit than any sign or manifestation or ecstasy or feeling or dream or emotion. To make such assertions only genders carnality, which results in contentions, etc. All this is made clear in the words which follow:

> That there should be no schism in the body; but that the members should have the same care one for another.
>
> And whether one member suffer, all the members suffer with it; or one member be honored, all the members rejoice with it.
>
> Now ye are the body of Christ, and members in particular (I Corinthians 12:25-27).

Oh, that we might learn the lesson of knowing our own gift and our own place, and our own service and fulfilling our responsibility without looking at or judging others or making our experience the pattern for anyone else. Well may we heed the words of Paul in the following verses;

> And God hath set some in the church, first apostles, secondarily prophets, thirdly teachers, after that miracles, then gifts of healings, helps, governments, diversities of tongues.
>
> Are all apostles? are all prophets? are all teachers? are all workers of miracles?
>
> Have all the gifts of healing? do all speak with tongues? do all interpret?
>
> But covet earnestly the best gifts: and yet show I unto you a more excellent way (I Corinthians 12:28-31).

Notice that in this enumeration of the gifts of the Spirit, tongues are mentioned last of all, and therefore, are the least of the gifts. But in Corinth they had headed the list.

In conclusion, therefore, let me remind you that the gift of tongues was most prominent in the most carnal of all the churches. God gave the gift to the weakest, most immature, childish believers at Corinth until they should grow up and become mature and have no more need for special manifestations. It is a significant fact that there is no mention of tongues made in any other epistle of Paul, only in this Epistle to the Corinthians. Tongues evidently were limited to the carnal infant church at Corinth. This was for a particular reason, and the reason was the immaturity of the Corinthian believers and their childlike condition in the faith. These Corinthians were not satisfied with just the simple promises of God. They wanted more evidence than the "Word of the Lord." Before they would believe, they wanted some physical or emotional or ecstatic experience, something they could see or feel or hear. They were still "babes in Christ."

But to the mature believer these things are wholly secondary. We believe upon the authority of the Word of God, because He who cannot lie has said it. Yes, God said it. I believe it and that settles it. All else belongs to spiritual infancy.

And to you who are not believers, are you too looking for a sign or a feeling or an emotion or a manifestation before you are willing to believe the Word of God? You will never be saved by believing signs or wonders or miracles or other sensory evidence, for salvation is entirely by faith in the promises of God. Our Lord Jesus Christ said:

> He that heareth my word, and believeth on him that sent me, hath everlasting life, and shall not come into condemnation; but is passed from death unto life (John 5:24).

In our coming message we shall see the reason why the Lord made a very special exception in the Corinthian church, in order to meet a need in their spiritual infancy.

*Chapter Twenty-two*

# TONGUES AND PENTECOST

> For God is not the author of confusion, but of peace, as in all churches of the saints (I Corinthians 14:33).
>
> Let all things be done decently and in order (I Corinthians 14:40).

THESE verses, written by Paul to the Corinthian church, were written to correct the terrible abuses connected with the speaking in tongues in the assembly of God. Unless such speaking is decent and orderly and profitable to the assembly, it cannot be of the Spirit of God. In I Corinthians 12, 13, and 14, Paul attempts to correct certain extremes and errors which were prevalent in Corinth with regard to this gift of tongues. He writes to correct the abuse of the gift, and not necessarily to endorse its universal use. God had given them this gift in all good faith because of their immaturity in grace and their ignorance of the Word of God. The Lord condescends, as it were, temporarily to give them this special evidence to bolster their weak faith. Remember, these Corinthians had only recently come out of paganism and were unfamiliar with the Word of God, and so lacked the background which many of the Jewish believers had enjoyed. As they grew to spiritual maturity, there would be less and less occasion for these special manifestations and signs and wonders.

But while the Lord gave these gifts to them in all good faith, they had abused them and the abuse had resulted in utter confusion and bedlam and disorder. And so Paul pleads with them, and concludes these three corrective chapters:

> Wherefore, brethren, covet to prophesy, and forbid not to speak with tongues (I Corinthians 14:39).

And then follows the closing warning, and incidently the solution to the entire problem:

> Let all things be done decently and in order (I Corinthians 14:40).

We take up now chapter 14. We are skipping over I Corinthians 13, because of its position between 12 and 14. Three whole chapters are devoted to the gift of tongues. The first of these three (I Corinthians 12) and the last of these (I Corinthians 14) are occupied with God's revelation concerning the proper use of the gift, in an effort to correct its unscriptural uses and abuses. Then, sandwiched and placed between these two chapters, we have chapter 13, which is the answer and the solution to the entire problem of these gifts.

Before taking up chapter 14, however, we must say one word about the incident in Acts, chapter 2, on the day of Pentecost. There the Apostles also spake in tongues.

> And they were all filled with the Holy Ghost, and began to speak with other tongues, as the Spirit gave them utterance . . .
> And they were all amazed and marveled, saying one to another, Behold, are not all these which speak Galileans?
> And how hear we every man in our own tongue, wherein we were born? (Acts 2:4, 7, 8).

Now this manifestation at the day of Pentecost was not the same as the gift of tongues in I Corinthians 12 and 14. The Apostles did not speak in *unknown* tongues, but in the known languages of the people to whom they spake. To confuse the Pentecostal speaking of tongues which was just for that one occasion, with the "sign" of tongues in I Corinthians, is totally to confuse and becloud the issue. The languages spoken at Pentecost were all languages spoken daily by the worshipers present from all over the world who had come together for the feast. They were not "unknown" tongues in any sense whatsoever, and were entirely different than the tongues in I Corinthians. They were a special provision for just this one single occasion at Pentecost so that all to whom the apostles spoke could hear and understand the Gospel.

The "Pentecostal" manifestation of tongues was never again repeated. If the Pentecostal gift of tongues were for us today, none of our missionaries would have to spend any time in language study. They could then go to a foreign land and immediately begin preaching to the people in their own language without any previous preparation. The Apostles did just this on the day of Pentecost. To those, therefore, who claim that the "Pentecostal" tongues are still for today, I would like to ask sincerely and honestly this question, Why must our missionaries spend months and years learning a foreign language? If this gift of tongues is for us, then I assert that the foreign missionary fields are the places for this manifestation and gift. It would not be just an ecstatic outburst once in a while among those who can't understand a word of it. I would like to emphasize this fact. All the Apostles spake in other languages and they needed "no interpreter":

>And how hear we every man in our own tongue, wherein we were born? (Acts 2:8).

## Not the Same

From this, therefore, it will be perfectly apparent that the apostolic speaking in tongues at Pentecost and the "sign" of tongues in Corinth have nothing in common at all; rather, they were two totally different experiences. If there is any profit in the speaking of tongues today, it certainly would be most evident in our missionary endeavor. But in spite of all the claims which are being made for this gift, the missionaries still must spend tiresome, tedious months and years in studying the language of the people whom they serve and then they never really become as proficient in it as the natives. We ask the question again in all sincerity: If this gift is for us today, why then does not the Lord give to those who have dedicated themselves to the service of the Lord, the ability to speak immediately in the language of the people to whom they have been commissioned.

And now for the teaching of Paul in I Corinthians 14.

Notice how different the "sign" of tongues in this passage.

Follow after charity, and desire spiritual gifts, but rather that ye may prophesy.

For he that speaketh in an unknown tongue speaketh not unto men, but unto God: for no man understandeth him; howbeit in the spirit he speaketh mysteries.

But he that prophesieth speaketh unto men to edification, and exhortation, and comfort.

He that speaketh in an unknown tongue edifieth himself; but he that prophesieth edifieth the church.

I would that ye all spake with tongues, but rather that ye prophesied: for greater is he that prophesieth than he that speaketh with tongues, except he interpret, that the church may receive edifying (I Corinthians 14:1-5).

The gift of tongues was one of the lesser gifts as will be seen in this passage. It is one of the least important. To prophesy (preach or testify, as well as predict) was a more excellent and important gift, but one that seemed to be neglected entirely in the Corinthian church, while the church sought the more spectacular but less important gift of tongues. In the list of the gifts of the Spirit in I Corinthians 12, the gifts of wisdom, faith, healing, miracles, prophecy are mentioned first, and the gift of tongues is mentioned only toward the very last. But the Corinthians had placed the "tongues" first and made it more important than all of the others, even to the neglect of the others. Their test whereby they judged everyone else was, "Do you speak in tongues?" It was to them the all important thing, although the Spirit had given it a much lesser and minor important place. This is the point of Paul's rebuke in verses 1 through 5.

But now Paul continues in his argument against the abuses in the Corinthian church concerning this gift,

Now, brethren, if I come unto you speaking with tongues, what shall I profit you, except I shall speak to you either by revelation, or by knowledge, or by prophesying, or by doctrine?

And even things without life giving sound, whether pipe or harp, except they give a distinction in the sounds, how shall it be known what is piped or harped?

> For if the trumpet give an uncertain sound, who shall pre-
> pare himself to the battle?
> So likewise ye, except ye utter by the tongue words easy
> to be understood, how shall it be known what is spoken? for
> ye shall speak into the air (I Corinthians 14:6-9).

Little needs to be added to these simple words which a child can understand. Whatever message is conveyed, either in tongues or in prophecy, must first of all be simple, it must be intelligible, and *easy* to understand. Moreover, it must be profitable and must contain doctrine. Merely some ecstatic statement which has no direct bearing upon the welfare of the church certainly cannot be of the Spirit of the Lord. Speaking was not to be a meaningless jibber-jabber of unintelligible confusing sounds. If the message cannot be understood, then says Paul, "Ye have become as sounding brass, or a tinkling cymbal" (I Corinthians 13:1b).

> Therefore if I know not the meaning of the voice, I shall
> be unto him that speaketh a barbarian, and he that speaketh
> shall be a barbarian unto me (I Corinthians 14:11).

Unless the tongues can be intelligibly interpreted in harmony with the Word of God, they are useless according to the words of Scripture. Notice, therefore, carefully verse 13:

> Wherefore let him that speaketh in an unknown tongue pray
> that he may interpret (I Corinthians 14:13).

The apostle Paul knew what he was talking about. He too spake in tongues. In fact he excelled them all in this gift for he says in verse 18:

> I thank my God, I speak with tongues more than ye all.

And yet while he could say this, there is no evidence that Paul ever used the gift. There is no other mention in all his epistles that he ever exercised this gift. He realized its minor importance and the danger of its abuses and gave it a subordinate position. No wonder that he goes on to say:

> Yet in the church I had rather speak five words with my
> understanding, that by my voice I might teach others also,
> than ten thousand words in an unknown tongue (I Cor. 14:19).

Paul was so impressed with the necessity of bearing testi-

mony and witnessing for the Lord Jesus Christ that he seems
to have used the gift of tongues on only rare occasions. He
certainly did not give it a place of prominence or make it the
test of fellowship or the test of salvation. While he spake in
tongues more than any of them, there is no indication that
he used it to interrupt his preaching of the Gospel.

## SIGN OF IMMATURITY

And now we come to the very heart of the matter. Paul
informs these Corinthians that the "sign" of tongues was God's
gracious provision for "infants" in the faith, and was not
intended for mature Christian believers. It is food for babies
who cannot yet stand solid meat. Signs and miracles belong
to spiritual infancy and childhood. How emphatically this
is stated in verse 20:

> Brethren, be not children in understanding: howbeit in
> malice be ye children, but in understanding be men.

The words here are unmistakable. Paul admonishes these
children, babes in Corinth, to grow up and to become mature
and to walk as men. He says in essence, Don't be children
all your lives. Grow up beyond these elementary things. God
gave you these signs because you were weak immature believers, as a temporary evidence, as a sort of a crutch for your
weak faith while you were developing from your spiritual
infancy to mature spiritual manhood. And that is the only
purpose for giving these "signs" to the Corinthian church.

In I Corinthians 13, which we study later, Paul says, with
reference to these primitive "signs":

> When I was a child, I spake as a child, I understood as a
> child, I thought as a child: but when I became a man, I put
> away childish things (I Corinthians 13:11).

Nothing pleases God more than to have His children believe His simple Word, without asking for anything else besides. Just trusting His promises without any other evidence,
manifestation or sign. To ask for anything more, over and

above God's promise in God's Word, is to admit that you cannot trust God just on the simple testimony of Scripture.

If I were to promise my son some valuable present on his next coming birthday, it would grieve my heart greatly as a father if he should demand some additional security. Suppose that he would say to me, "I believe that you are going to give me this gift on my next birthday, but I would like to be in possession of more assurance. I wish that you would make that promise legal in writing or I wish that you would deposit the money for it in my name." You know how I would feel about this; I would be deeply grieved because my own son did not believe me on the simple promise of my word alone. So, too, it must grieve the father's heart to have his children expect or demand some witness of the Spirit in feelings, signs, emotions, visions, dreams, or any other evidence besides the simple promises of His Word. I have committed my soul for eternity to the Word and the promise of God. He said,

For whosoever shall call upon the name of the Lord shall be saved (Romans 10:13).

And by the grace of God I did this many years ago, and I believe with all my heart that God will keep His promise even though I may not have any additional evidence at all. Nothing can please the heart of the Lord more than for us to take Him at His Word and to trust for our salvation entirely in the "thus saith the Lord."

This is God's way of salvation. This is God's only way of salvation, and so God expects every sinner to come to the Lord Jesus Christ, "believing" what God has to say about his hopeless, lost condition and then believing the record of God's provision in the finished work of the Lord Jesus Christ. I need no other evidence.

*Chapter Twenty-three*

## SPEAKING IN TONGUES

> Wherefore tongues are for a sign, not to them that believe,
> but to them that believe not: but prophesying serveth not for
> them that believe not, but for them which believe (I Corin-
> thians 14:22).

THIS verse is the heart of Paul's discussion of the gift of
tongues as it was present and manifested in the church of
Corinth. We remind you again that the church at Corinth
seems to be the only one to whom God in any great measure
gave these peculiar and definite gifts of the Spirit. There is
no mention of "speaking in tongues" in any of the other
epistles of Paul or, in fact, in any of the other epistles of the
New Testament. In the previous verses Paul had given certain
instructions for the decent and orderly use of this gift as it
was exercised in the church of Corinth, and now he goes on
to give the reason why God gave this sign so abundantly in
this particular church. In no other church, we repeat, in the
New Testament do we find this same problem. It is only in
the church at Corinth where tongues were abundant and
abused.

### THE CARNAL CHURCH

The reason for this is simple. The Corinthians were "babes"
in Christ. They were weaklings, and being unskillful in the
Word of God, and as Gentiles ignorant of the Scriptures, the
Lord gave them these signs as a sort of a crutch and a help
until they were more mature and grown up. This is definitely
implied in the Scripture we referred to in verse 20 of our
chapter:

153

Brethren, be not children in understanding: howbeit in malice be ye children, but in understanding be men (I Corinthians 14:20).

Paul definitely infers here that these signs were given to those who were still babes in their understanding of the full truth of the grace of God. Tongues in Corinth were for folks with weak faith. Paul says so in verse 22:

Wherefore tongues are for a sign not to them that believe, but to them that believe not (I Corinthians 14:22).

We must stop right here because these words are important and hold the key to the entire situation. First of all, Paul is talking only about born-again believers. It is important to remember this. No unconverted person can have the genuine gift of tongues or any other genuine gift of the Spirit, for it is a spiritual gift and the unbeliever is spiritually dead. So let us remember that he is talking to born-again believers only. But he divides these Christian, born-again believers into two groups. "Those saints who believe" and "those saints who believe not." Two different words are used in the Greek. The word used in the first phrase, "tongues are for a sign, not to them that believe . . ." (I Corinthians 14:22). is the word *pisteuo*, which denotes full confidence and trust. In the second instance, in the phrase, "but to them that believe not . . ." (I Corinthians 14:22), the word is *apistos* and means one who does not fully trust. It may be translated "doubter," so that the passage would naturally read,

Wherefore tongues are for a sign, not to them [who fully trust the Lord], but to them [who still doubt] (I Corinthians 14:22).

To those who ask for no other evidence than the promises of God and the Word of God alone, signs become wholly unnecessary. If the Lord pleases to give them, well and good, but they are not to be expected. And these Corinthians were still largely ignorant of the promises of the Word of God, and so the Lord stoops to give them some additional evidence. The Lord as it were accommodates Himself to their weakness in order to bolster their weak and childish faith. Paul, therefore, pleads with these carnal Corinthians to believe and fully trust the Lord and not be so unbelieving as to demand signs and miracles and other manifestations before they fully trust His Word.

An illustration of how the Lord condescends to meet man's weak faith is in John 20:24-29. Jesus had appeared to the disciples after His resurrection. Thomas the doubter was absent, and upon hearing the testimony of the other disciples exclaimed, I will not believe it except I see. Here are his exact words:

> Except I shall see in his hands the print of the nails, and put my finger into the print of the nails, and thrust my hand into his side, I will not believe (John 20:25).

Thomas wanted additional evidence. He wanted to see and to feel. He wanted to see the wounds, and he wanted to feel the side of the Lord Jesus. And then after seven days the Lord appears again with Thomas present; and our Lord, instead of castigating Thomas, stoops to his weak faith and says to Thomas:

> Reach hither thy finger, and behold my hands; and reach hither thy hand, and thrust it into my side: and be not faithless, but believing (John 20:27).

The Lord Jesus recognized the little faith of Thomas and his weak trust and granted him his demand to see and to feel, but then He adds:

> . . . and be not faithless, but believing (John 20:27).

The word "faithless" is a translation of the same word which in I Corinthians 14:22 is used concerning those who "believe not." The word is *apistos.* The word translated "faithless" and "believe not" does not mean that they were not saved and did not have saving faith. But it means instead that these believers were still weak in their faith and did not fully trust the Lord. Certainly Thomas was saved, but he was faithless in the matter of believing the simple testimony of the disciples and in asking for additional evidence. He demanded additional manifestation, and the Lord stoops to accommodate him, but then warns him that it is not the ideal way and says:

> . . . and be not faithless, but believing (John 20:27).

And then to clinch it all the Lord says to him,

> Thomas, because thou hast seen me, thou hast believed: blessed are they that have not seen, and yet have believed (John 20:29).

It is better to believe the Lord without any further evidence than the testimony of His Word, than to distrust the Lord because of the lack of feelings or emotions or other manifestations.

### FOR BABES IN CHRIST

This then is the answer to the tongues question. It explains why tongues were so prevalent in Corinth and not in the other churches. If there is any such thing as the gift of tongues today, it is still reserved for those who are immature and untaught spiritually. We do not say that God cannot give this gift of tongues today, for all things are possible with God. We believe, however, as we shall show in our coming message that it ceased as a common gift with the close of the Apostolic Age. But we repeat, if the gift of tongues is given to anyone today, then let us remember that it is a mark of spiritual infancy. To the mature believer God's promises are all sufficient. God says it, I believe it, that settles it. Abraham believed God and it was counted unto him for righteousness.

> He that believeth on the Son of God hath the witness in himself: he that believeth not God hath made him a liar; because he believeth not the record that God gave of his Son (I John 5:10).

Nothing can so please the Lord as believing the simple record of the Word of God, and not looking for any other additional evidence.

### DETAILED INSTRUCTIONS

This chapter closes with a number of instructions by Paul regarding the control of the gift of tongues. In verses 23 to

28 he gives the orderliness with which the church should exercise everyone of its God-given gifts.

> If therefore the whole church be come together into one place, and all speak with tongues, and there come in those that are unlearned, or unbelievers, will they not say that ye are mad?
>
> How is it then, brethren? when ye come together, every one of you hath a psalm, hath a doctrine, hath a tongue, hath a revelation, hath an interpretation. Let all things be done unto edifying (I Corinthians 14:23, 26).

What a scene of confusion this presents to us. Everyone wanted to be heard and to be seen. Instead of waiting for one another and carrying on the service in orderliness, all seemed to have talked at once, each one striving to be heard and seen above the others, and the result was that all one could hear was bedlam, disorder and confusion of tongues. And so Paul says:

> If any man speak in an unknown tongue, let it be by two, or at the most by three, and that by course [not all together]; and let one interpret.
>
> But if there be no interpreter, let him keep silence in the church; and let him speak to himself, and to God (I Corinthians 14:27, 28).

No more than two or three were to speak at any one church service. And they must wait for one another. That is the meaning of the expression "by course." And one must always be able to interpret. Otherwise it is better to keep still. There was to be no interrupting of one another, no babble of several voices, no confusion of any kind. The same was true of the gift of prophecy also (verses 29-32). The reason is clear in verse 33:

> For God is not the author of confusion, but of peace, as in all churches of the saints (I Corinthians 14:33).

## WOMEN KEEP SILENT

But now notice another corrective measure which Paul suggests when he says,

> Let your women keep silence in the churches: for it is not

permitted unto them to speak; but they are commanded to be under obedience, as also saith the law.

And if they will learn any thing, let them ask their husbands at home: for it is a shame for women to speak in the church (I Corinthians 14:34, 35).

We must again remember the setting of this passage. It has reference primarily to the women speaking in tongues; it does not refer to the testimonies or the prayers of women. But the admonition is definite and positive and unmistakable that the speaking of tongues is reserved in the Corinthian church for the men only and is never to be exercised by the women. Wherever the use of tongues by women occurs it is not according to the Word, and therefore, must be a counterfeit.

### Conclusion

And so Paul concludes this section of Corinthians with a word of warning:

And if they [the women] will learn any thing, let them ask their husbands at home: for it is a shame for women to speak in the church.

What came the word of God out from you? or came it unto you only?

If any man think himself to be a prophet, or spiritual, let him acknowledge that the things that I write unto you are the commandments of the Lord.

But if any man be ignorant, let him be ignorant.

Wherefore, brethren, covet to prophesy, and forbid not to speak with tongues.

Let all things be done decently and in order (I Corinthians 14:35-40).

Paul does not therefore give to the Corinthian church a prohibition against speaking in tongues, but the speaking must measure up to the requirements laid down by the apostle in these chapters and must always be done decently and in order. And so before closing this chapter, let me again sum up the teaching of Paul.

1. The sign of tongues was a gift of the Holy Spirit to the Corinthian church particularly.

2. It was more prevalent in the Corinthian church than in any other church, if not exclusively present in Corinth.

3. It was a special dispensation to weak and untaught believers. The Lord stooped to give them extra evidence because of their ignorance of His Word.

4. This gift was not for every one, but only a special number, according to God's own will.

5. It was never to be used unless it could be interpreted.

6. It was the least important of all the gifts.

7. No more than two or three were allowed to speak at any one of the services.

8. It must be done without disorder or confusion.

9. It was for men only. The women were to keep silence in the churches.

10. It was only for a limited time and ceased after the church had the complete Bible. It was an apostolic gift which ceased after the Apostolic Age.

11. God is far more pleased when we rest our assurance of salvation on the witness of the Holy Spirit in His Word than when we depend upon signs and wonders.

We repeat again the words of our Lord Jesus to Thomas, . . . because thou hast seen me, thou hast believed: blessed are they that have not seen, and yet have believed (John 20:29).

*Chapter Twenty-four*

# TONGUES SHALL CEASE

> Though I speak with the tongues of men and of angels, and have not [love], I am become as sounding brass, or a tinkling cymbal (I Corinthians 13:1).

THIS is the opening verse of one of the best known and most often quoted chapters in the New Testament. It is commonly called "The Great Love Chapter." However it should properly be called "The Great Tongues Chapter." It is placed between the two great chapters which deal with the gift of speaking in tongues (I Cor. 12 and I Cor. 14). It is the Holy Spirit's own inspired answer to the problem of the gifts of the Spirit in the Corinthian church. While this chapter exalts the necessity and the pre-eminence of love in the believer's conduct and in the life of the Christian, it it only introduced to show by contrast how inferior to love are the gifts of the Spirit and especially the lesser gift of tongues.

Paul in I Corinthians 12 had pointed out the place of tongues in the church and bemoaned the sad fact that such undue importance and prominence had been given to this gift. Then he concludes the chapter with:

> Have all the gifts of healing? do all speak with tongues? do all interpret?
> But covet earnestly the best gifts: and yet show I unto you a more excellent way (I Corinthians 12:30, 31).

It is only then that chapter 13 opens with:

> Though I speak with the tongues of men and of angels, and have not [love], I am become as sounding brass, or a tinkling cymbal (I Corinthians 13:1).

There should, of course, never have been any break between chapter 12 and chapter 13. Thirteen is a continuation of chapter 12 and the explanation of the matters discussed in this chapter.

## The Greatest Gift

Any gift which does not provoke love and tolerance and forbearance toward other believers is not a gift from the Lord. The real test of all the gifts of the Spirit is whether they promote love and understanding and regard for our fellow believers. There are those who tell us that the "witness" of the Holy Spirit is found in the speaking of tongues or having revelations or performing miracles. However, there is not a verse in the Scriptures on which to base such a carnal self-righteous statement. If one's special gift makes one critical and censorious and proud and faultfinding, it certainly is not a gift of the Holy Spirit. The Bible is clear that:

The fruit of the Spirit is love, joy, peace . . . (Galatians 5:22).

Nowhere does it say that other manifestations are the fruit of the Spirit. Love is the final and acid test. And so Paul says that even though he had all of the gifts of the Spirit — miracles, prophecy, tongues, knowledge, wisdom — and yet lacked love, it would be utterly useless. Listen to Paul:

And though I have the gift of prophecy, and understand all mysteries, and all knowledge; and though I have all faith, so that I could remove mountains, and have not [love], I am nothing.

And though I bestow all my goods to feed the poor, and though I give my body to be burned, and have not [love], it profiteth me nothing.

[Love] suffereth long, and is kind; [love] envieth not; [love] vaunteth not itself, is not puffed up,

Doth not behave itself unseemly, seeketh not her own, is not easily provoked, thinketh no evil;

Rejoiceth not in iniquity, but rejoiceth in the truth;

Beareth all things, believeth all things, hopeth all things, endureth all things (I Corinthians 13:2-7).

## LOVE NEVER FAILS

But the climaxing characteristic of love is its permanency and its lasting nature. It is not for a certain time only, or for a special occasion, or for a single church, or for one individual. It is for everyone, for every age, and for every circumstance. This is not true of the gift of tongues or the other gifts of the Spirit. The gift of tongues seemed very largely to be confined to the church in Corinth, the childish carnal church among the churches of the New Testament. And the gift of tongues too was not permanent. It was to cease when its purpose was fulfilled in the council of God. Listen to the words:

> [Love] never faileth: but whether there be prophecies, they shall fail; whether there be tongues, they shall cease; whether there be knowledge, it shall vanish away (I Corinthians 13:8).

Here, then, we have the answer to the apostolic gifts of the first century. They were temporary in their nature and for a limited time only and only for a special occasion. Remember, the only Scriptures the Corinthians had access to were the Old Testament books. They did not yet have a single book of the New Testament as far as we know. Revelation was still incomplete, and so until the complete Bible was available and the perfect revelation of God in the Scriptures had been fully given, the Lord gave these gifts of the Spirit as a temporary provision until the canon of Scripture should be completed. How else could the Spirit of God make known His will and teach these new Christians? God, therefore, gave certain ones in the church who should receive special revelations, gifts of prophecy and the revealing of new truth, and tongues to edify the church. All this was in view of the fact that the Scriptures with their complete revelation were not yet available.

But after all the books of the Bible were written and the revelation was complete there was no longer any need for such special demonstrations. The Bible itself is a sufficient and full revelation of God's plan and purpose for every believer's life, so that there can be no more need for any additional revelation. God expects us to be satisfied and content with that which is contained between the covers of this sacred Book.

## TONGUES SHALL CEASE

And this our Scripture plainly asserts:

> Love never faileth: but whether there be prophecies, they shall fail (I Corinthians 13:8a).

The word translated "faileth" in this particular passage in the original means "to drop away," so that Paul says, Love as a permanent gift shall never drop away, but whether there be prophecies, they shall "fail." But the word "fail" in the phrase as applied to prophecies is quite another word. The word is *katargeo* and my lexicon translates it as "to render entirely unnecessary." The gift of prophecy, present in the Corinthian church to give new revelation while the Bible was still incomplete, would be rendered entirely unnecessary upon the completion of the Scriptures. Since the close, therefore, of Revelation 22, there has been no additional revelation necessary. The Spirit gives illumination to believers to discover in the Bible new truths not seen before, but the truths have been there all the time. We, therefore, claim illumination of the Spirit of God, but no man has a right to claim revelation of a new truth, one not contained in the Word of God, because the Bible has been completed. Every thing God wants us to know is in this Book, and there is no need for additional revelation or evidence. The Bible itself closes with a very solemn and stern warning against adding anything to that which is already contained in the Word:

> If any man shall add unto these things, God shall add unto him the plagues that are written in this book. (Revelation 22:18b).

## TRUE OF ALL GIFTS

That which is true of prophecies is also true of the other gifts of the Spirit which were present in the Church:

Whether there be tongues, they shall cease; whether there be knowledge [special knowledge of unrevealed truth], it shall vanish away (I Corinthians 13:8).

Tongues, therefore, shall cease. The word "cease" in the original is *pauo* and means literally "to come to a complete stop." Could anything be clearer in the Word of God. And so we can translate the verse without doing violence to the text:

Love never drops away, but whether there be prophecies, they shall be rendered unnecessary, whether there be tongues, they shall come to a complete stop; whether there be the spiritual gift of knowledge, it shall vanish away (I Corinthians 13:8, free translation).

The next verses which follow explain all of this and prove it to be the proper explanation:

For we know in part [incompletely], and we prophesy in part [while the Word was still incomplete].

But when that which is perfect is come, then that which is in part [or incomplete] shall be done away (I Corinthians 13:9, 10).

When that which is perfect is come, the completed Scriptures, then that which is in part or incomplete shall be done away. When the Scripture is completed with the writing of the last book of the Bible, then that which was in part shall cease to have its place in the life of the believer. It is the end of special signs, given during the infancy of the Church. The imperfect must give way to the perfect.

## For Children

These gifts, then, were for the young infant Church before revelation was complete. Tongues belong to spiritual childhood. They were present in the early Church, and so Paul says,

When that which is perfect is come, then that which is in part shall be done away (I Corinthians 13:10).

The word "perfect" here, as in other passages of Scripture, would more properly be translated "maturity," and so what Paul says is that when maturity of the Church has been attained, then that which is incomplete and temporary shall be done away. This is all made clear in the following verses:

> When I was a child, I spake as a child, I understood as a child, I thought as a child: but when I became a man, I put away childish things.
>
> For now we see through a glass, darkly; but then face to face: now I know in part; but then shall I know even as also I am known (I Corinthians 13:11, 12).

"When I was a child, I spake as a child." We must remember that Paul is still speaking about the gifts of the Spirit and particularly about the gift of tongues. But now since the complete revelation of God is ours, we have put away these childish things, and find in the Word of God all and everything that we need for salvation, sanctification, joy and service, and we ask for no more from the Lord.

Till revelation was complete believers saw through a glass darkly, but now we have the full face-to-face revelation of the Lord Jesus in the Word. We now not only have part of the Bible and therefore know in part, but we now have all of the Bible so that we may know, as we are known.

Our Lord wants us to be mature saints of God, not little children. The special temporary gifts were for little children, the abiding permanent gifts are for mature believers. And so we read in Ephesians 4:11, where Paul is writing to the mature church at Ephesus:

> And he gave some, apostles; and some, prophets; and some, evangelists; and some, pastors and teachers;
>
> For the perfecting [maturing] of the saints, for the work of the ministry, for the edifying of the body of Christ:
>
> Till we all come in the unity of the faith, and of the knowledge of the Son of God, unto a perfect [mature] man, unto the measure of the fulness of Christ:
>
> That we henceforth be no more children, tossed to and fro, and carried about with every wind of doctrine, by the sleight of men, and cunning craftiness, whereby they lie in wait to deceive;
>
> But speaking the truth in love, may grow up into him in all things, which is the head, even Christ (Ephesians 4:11-15).

Speaking the truth in "love" is far more important than speaking the truth in "tongues." Jesus Himself said,

> By this shall all men know that ye are my disciples, if ye have love one to another (John 13:35).

Any gift or manifestation claiming to be from the Spirit of God which does not make us loving and kind and tender and considerate toward our fellow believers, is certainly not of the Lord. The Lord wants us to be mature and to be strong and to acquit ourselves like men.

That is just exactly what we of the Radio Bible Class are trying to do. We are trying to speak the truth in love, but speak it firmly no matter where the chips may fall. We believe the only shield against all of the strange and unscriptural movements of this day is a thorough knowledge of the Word of God. Only as we are grounded in the Book will we be foolproof against the deceptions of this age and be able to *grow up in Him.* That is why we carry on a strictly Bible-teaching ministry. We would like to quote Ephesians 6:13:

> Wherefore take unto you the whole armour of God, that ye may be able to withstand in the evil day, and having done all, to stand.

It is not an easy matter to stand fast and firm and unmoved in the Gospel of God's grace in these days with so much false doctrine and many strange teachings of men. The only way we can stand is to be firmly grounded and rooted in the Word of the living God and to know what the perfect and acceptable will of God is in our lives.

> Study to shew thyself approved unto God, a workman that needeth not to be ashamed, rightly dividing the word of truth (II Timothy 2:15).

*Chapter Twenty-five*

# THE GOSPEL OF THE RESURRECTION

> Moreover, brethren, I declare unto you the gospel which
> I preached unto you, which also ye have received, and wherein
> ye stand;
> By which also ye are saved, if ye keep in memory what I
> preached unto you, unless ye have believed in vain.
> For I delivered unto you first of all that which I also re-
> ceived, how that Christ died for our sins according to the
> scriptures;
> And that he was buried, and that he rose again the third
> day according to the scriptures (I Corinthians 15:1-4).

THE gospel means "good news." According to Paul it is
the good news concerning the death and the resurrection of
Jesus Christ. This indeed is good news for the sinner. Man
by nature is lost, depraved, helpless and hopeless. But God
sent His Son to bear our sins on the Cross, and declared His
complete satisfaction with the work of the Son of God by
raising Him from the dead on the third day. And now the
poor, hopeless, helpless sinner can be saved, simply by receiving in faith the finished work of the Lord Jesus Christ.
This indeed is good news to a helpless sinner.

### RESURRECTION IMPORTANT

The good news of the Gospel is not only the death of
Christ. The Cross alone is bad news. Only the resurrection
makes it good news. For had Christ failed to atone for every
single sin His death would have been an absolute failure, for
He would have remained in death. If one single sin of
mankind which God laid upon Christ had been left unpaid,

Christ could never have arisen from the dead. The Bible plainly declares:

> . . . the wages of sin is death (Romans 6:23).

One single sin, therefore, was enough to demand eternal death. But by the resurrection of Jesus Christ we are assured that every sin was paid. God's demands were fully met and the work indeed is finished.

The Gospel, therefore, is the message of the death and particularly the resurrection of Christ. Paul, therefore, devotes one entire chapter in I Corinthians to the important doctrine of the resurrection. There seem to have been some in the Corinthian church who questioned the resurrection, and they had informed Paul about it, and so he leaves this important subject as the last matter which he seeks to correct in the assembly.

The chapter divides itself automatically into five definite sections:

1. The proof of the resurrection (verses 1-11).
2. The importance of the resurrection (verses 12-19).
3. The order of the resurrection (verses 20-34).
4. The nature of our resurrection bodies (verses 35-50).
5. The time of the resurrection (verses 51-58).

Just a few comments on each of these sections. The proofs of the resurrection are so numerous that no one can face them and remain unconvinced, unless he is totally and spiritually blind. Luke says in Acts 1 that Jesus shewed Himself alive by "many infallible proofs" (Acts 1:3). Paul names some of these proofs and says that:

> He was seen of Cephas, then of the twelve:
> After that, he was seen of above five hundred brethren at once: of whom the greater part remain unto this present, but some are fallen asleep.
> After that, he was seen of James; then of all the apostles.
> And last of all he was seen of me also, as of one born out of due time (I Corinthians 15:5-8).

He mentions only a few of those who saw the Lord after

His resurrection. He does not mention the women or the two disciples on the way to Emmaus, but he does mention enough witnesses, living witnesses, still alive when Paul wrote this epistle to beat down any denial of the literal resurrection of the Lord Jesus.

We call special attention to Paul's statement that Jesus was seen after the resurrection by above five hundred brethren at one time, of whom most were still alive during Paul's day. Paul does not tell us on what occasion this happened, but he is bold in making the assertion that most of them were still alive and therefore could be contacted as to their experience of this event. This was, therefore, an unassailable testimony, for if Jesus had not risen, they had but to challenge Paul to produce these several hundred witnesses; but no such challenge was ever attempted.

And then finally, Paul says, "I myself saw him." He refers to his experience on the Damascus Road. He saw Christ in the glory, and His dazzling brilliance struck him blind until he was healed by Ananias. Yes, Paul knew that Christ was alive and had risen from the dead, for he had seen Him face to face. And all of us who have seen Him with the eye of faith in the Word of God know also that we serve a living Saviour.

## ANSWER TO DOUBT

The next thing which Paul proceeds to show is the importance of the resurrection:

> Now if Christ be preached that he rose from the dead, how say some among you that there is no resurrection of the dead? (I Corinthians 15:12).

There were evidently those who taught that there was no bodily resurrection, and they had led many of the Corinthian believers astray. Therefore, in a masterful argument Paul settles the matter in the following verses:

> But if there be no resurrection of the dead, then is Christ not risen (I Corinthians 15:13).

To deny a resurrection is to deny the resurrection of the

Lord Jesus. It makes Christ a liar, the apostle a deceiver, the Bible a fable and salvation a farce. Listen, therefore, to the words of Paul:

> And if Christ be not risen, then is our preaching vain, and your faith is also vain.
>
> Yea, and we are found false witnesses of God; because we have testified of God that he raised up Christ: whom he raised not up, if so be that the dead rise not.
>
> For if the dead rise not, then is not Christ raised:
>
> And if Christ be not raised, your faith is vain; ye are yet in your sins.
>
> Then they also which are fallen asleep in Christ are perished.
>
> If in this life only we have hope in Christ, we are of all men most miserable (I Corinthians 15:14-19).

Everything, therefore, in our Christian religion stands or falls with the literal resurrection of the Lord Jesus Christ from the grave. Could it be proved for one moment that Jesus never rose, the whole system of Christian religion would crumble in the dust. The resurrection is the keystone, the arch of our Christian faith. Without it, all is in vain. The modern practice of some who extol the wonderful life and teachings of Christ, and exalt His death as a martyr and example of a noble cause, and then deny His resurrection, is a contradiction, a farce, and a paradox. If Christ did not arise from the dead, He was a poor mistaken dupe, or a deliberate imposter. How could we exalt and extol the life and the death of such a One who claimed all this for Himself, if He were unable to make good His claims.

### DEATH PLUS RESURRECTION

To preach the Cross alone is not the Gospel. To proclaim the substitutionary death of Christ for sinners is not the full story of salvation. The Gospel can be no Gospel without the resurrection. If there be no resurrection, then the life of Christ ended in tragedy and His ignominious death on the Cross of Calvary is anything but good news. And yet how little we hear about the resurrection of Christ apart from the Easter

Season and a few special occasions. We preach the Cross, the Cross, the Cross, the wonderful death of the Saviour, and then bury Him and leave Him in the tomb. No sermon, therefore, can be called a gospel sermon which does not clearly proclaim Christ risen from the dead. And so Paul says:

> If in this life only we have hope in Christ, we are of all men most miserable (I Corinthians 15:19).

What fools we are proved to be for warning men and women to prepare for the afterlife if there be no resurrection. What infamous, despicable sadists we then become for scaring men and women with a future place of punishment if there be no resurrection. Remove the resurrection and we are left without hope of the future, and without a message.

### But Now

> But now is Christ risen from the dead, and become the first-fruits of them that slept.
>
> For since by man came death, by man came also the resurrection of the dead.
>
> For as in Adam all die, even so in Christ shall all be made alive (I Corinthians 15:20-22).

The resurrection of Christ, therefore, assures and guarantees the future resurrection of all men, both the saved and the lost. Adam as the federal head of the human race brought death, physical as well as spiritual death, upon all men. Jesus Christ, as the second man, the last Adam, made possible the physical resurrection of all of Adam's offspring, both the saved and the lost. Without the resurrection of Christ, no one would ever be raised from the dead, but as a result of His resurrection all men will someday be bodily raised. Their destiny will be different to be sure, but all, both saved and lost, will be resurrected bodily to exist forever, body and soul, either in heaven or in hell.

### A Solemn Thought

Man was created to live forever, and the fact that sin came and brought death does not put an end to God's purpose that man should live forever. All will be raised and all men both saved and lost will live forever. But while all will be raised to live forever they will not all have *eternal* life. There is a vast difference between existing forever, and having eternal life. Endless existence is quantitative. Eternal life is the life of God. It is not only endless existence, but beginningless existence, for it is the divine life of God imparted to the believer. This life is received only by faith in the death and the resurrection of the Lord Jesus. To reject Him means the "second death," which is eternal, spiritual, separation from God, but in no sense implies a cessation of existence. We, therefore, would like to call attention before we close to the words of the Lord Jesus in John 5:28. These words have a definite and direct bearing upon the words of Paul:

> Marvel not at this: for the hour is coming, in the which all that are in the graves shall hear his voice,
>
> And shall come forth; they that have done good, unto the resurrection of life; and they that have done evil, unto the resurrection of damnation (John 5:28, 29).

If there were no other Scripture in the entire Bible bearing on the fact of the resurrection this would be enough to establish four things. Notice these four things which the Lord definitely and unmistakably asserts:

1. There will be a resurrection.
2. It will be a resurrection of all men, for Jesus says, "All that are in the graves shall come forth."
3. It will be a bodily resurrection, for our Lord asserts here that the part of man which is in the grave shall come forth, and we know that the soul is not in the grave, but the body is that which reposes in the dust.
4. The resurrected will consist of two companies: those who have done good, unto the resurrection of life; and they that have done evil, unto the resurrection of damnation.

You, my friend, belong to this great company of those who shall be resurrected some time in the future. But how different will be the resurrection for those who have believed the Gospel from what it will be for those who have rejected it. The Lord says the one is a resurrection unto "life" and the other is a resurrection unto "damnation," and the entire issue rests upon faith in the One who was the first-begotten from the dead.

Jesus Christ was the first man in all of human history who arose from the dead, never to die again. There are instances of raising the dead in the Old Testament, and in the record of the Gospels, but we believe on the basis of the fact that Christ is the "first-fruits" of all resurrected ones that these individuals were revived from death with their natural bodies and subsequently died again and will be resurrected in glorified bodies sometime in the future. How else could Jesus be the first fruits of the resurrection? The Bible is absolutely silent as to the subsequent death of those few individuals who were raised from the dead before the resurrection of Christ, but it is evident that only those who were raised with Christ at His resurrection were raised never to die again.

What is your destiny? The saved will spend eternity with the resurrected Christ in heaven. The lost will spend eternity with the author of death, the Devil, in the place of eternal separation from God. The decision is up to you.

> He that believeth on him is not condemned: but he that believeth not is condemned already, because he hath not believed in the name of the only begotten Son of God (John 5:18).

*Chapter Twenty-six*

# THE FIRST RESURRECTION

> For as in Adam all die, even so in Christ shall all be made alive.
>
> But every man in his own order: Christ the firstfruits; afterward they that are Christ's at his coming.
>
> Then cometh the end, when he shall have delivered up the kingdom to God, even the Father; when he shall have put down all rule and all authority and power.
>
> For he must reign, till he hath put all enemies under his feet (I Corinthians 15:22-25).

THE Bible teaches life after death. It also teaches that this life will be in a body which will be raised from the grave. Jesus said in John 5:28, 29 that "all that are in the graves shall hear his voice and shall come forth," and thereby establishes immediately the fact of a universal resurrection of all those who have been born into the world.

As we have pointed out, the Lord establishes four things in these verses in John:

1. There will be a resurrection.
2. It will be a bodily resurrection and not a spiritual one.
3. It will include *all* men.
4. There will be two classes in this resurrection.

### Separated By Time

But the Bible further teaches that the saved and the lost will not be raised at the identical time and at the same moment. In I Thessalonians 4 we are told that the dead "in" Christ shall rise first, implying that those who are "out" of Christ shall not rise until later. In Revelation 20, we are told that a thousand years will separate these two resurrections. After describing the first resurrection of the blessed saved, John in Revelation says:

> But the rest of the dead lived not again until the thousand years were finished (Revelation 20:5).

A thousand years is a millennium and so we may read:

> But the rest of the dead lived not again until after the millennium (Revelation 20:5).

## AGREES WITH PAUL

The apostle Paul in I Corinthians 15 gives some added detail. He says that while all men will be raised ultimately, they will be raised at different times and under different circumstances. He mentions at least three groups in verses 23 and 24:

1. Christ the first fruits (this happened 1900 years ago).
2. Afterwards they that are Christ's at His coming (this is the next event).
3. Then cometh the end (or literally, "then the last ones").

Notice first of all that Christ is the first fruits of all resurrections. At the resurrection of the Lord Jesus a great host of Old Testament saints were also raised from the dead and were seen upon the streets of Jerusalem. In Matthew 27:52 we read:

> And the graves were opened; and many bodies [not all, but many] of the saints which slept arose,
>
> And came out of the graves after his [Jesus] resurrection, and went into the holy city, and appeared unto many (Matthew 27:52, 53).

These Old Testament saints, therefore, with Christ in resurrection bodies are in heaven today as the first fruits, and the earnest of the coming resurrection. Paul says, "Each one in his own order." The word "order" is a military term and means a company or a rank. The resurrection, therefore, will occur in separate companies. The first company was this group of

Old Testament saints who were raised at the time of the resurrection of Jesus.

However, the second group will be added to this first group of the first fruits when Jesus shouts from the air at the time of the rapture. In I Thessalonians 4 we have this company minutely described:

> For the Lord himself shall descend from heaven with a shout, with the voice of the archangel, and with the trump of God: and the dead in Christ shall rise first (I Thessalonians 4:16).

This, then, is the harvest of the resurrection at Jesus' coming, and to this company will later be added the tribulation saints described in Revelation 20, thus completing the first resurrection. In this first resurrection, consisting of the first fruits and those resurrected at Jesus' return plus the tribulation saints, only saved individuals will share. There will not be a single lost sinner resurrected until much later. These resurrected saints, however, are raised before the millennial reign of Christ, for we are definitely told that they "lived and reigned with Christ a thousand years."

## THE END ONES

And then Paul continues with the last group and says:

> Then *cometh* the end (I Corinthians 15:24a).

The word "cometh" is not in the original text as may be seen from the fact that it is written in italics, indicating that it was added by the translators. The text should then read properly:

> Christ the firstfruits; afterward they that are Christ's at his coming.
> Then the end [ones] . . . (I Corinthians 15:23, 24).

Now who are these last ones or these "end ones"? The Bible gives the answer clearly. Paul says that the resurrection of these "end ones" or "last ones" will occur after the Kingdom Age of Christ. He states it plainly in these words in our chapter:

> When he [Christ] shall have delivered up [past tense] the kingdom to God, even the Father; when he shall have put

down all rule, and all authority and power (I Corinthians 15:24).

It will therefore be after the final rebellion of Gog and Magog and the uprising of Satan at the close of the thousand-year reign of the Lord Jesus Christ. This is further clinched by the verse already referred to in Revelation 20:

> But the rest of the dead [the wicked dead] lived not again until the thousand years were finished (Rev. 20:5).

All these, therefore, in this last resurrection, described as the end ones, will then be judged at the great white throne and their place assigned in the lake of fire. This is the divine revelation. The first company of resurrected believers have already been in heaven for 1900 years as the earnest and the first fruits of our resurrection. Soon, we believe, the saints who have died since will join them at the rapture, and then seven years later the tribulation saints will complete the resurrection of all saved believers. And then will follow the thousand years of Christ's millennial reign in His kingdom with His saints, and then at the end all of the wicked dead will finally be raised.

This is the evident meaning of Paul's words, "But each in his own order [or company]." The Bible knows no such thing as a general resurrection at the end of the world. The saints of God shall never appear at the judgment of the great white throne. When that occurs they will already have been with the Lord in perfect safety for one thousand blessed years. And then eternity will come, or as Paul says in verse 28:

> And when all things shall be subdued unto him, then shall the Son also himself be subject unto him that put all things under him, that God may be all in all (I Corinthians 15:28).

## PAUL BELIEVED THIS

The apostle Paul evidently believed this with his whole heart and asserted that without this assurance every thing else would be hopeless. Listen to his words again:

> Else what shall they do which are baptized for the dead,

if the dead rise not at all? why are they then baptized for
the dead? (I Corinthians 15:29).

Now this verse has confused many, and various interpretations have been put forth. We believe that it means simply that if there was no resurrection, then what was the value
in professing Christ in the waters of baptism in view of coming death. In the days of Paul, Christians who declared themselves openly for Christ by submitting to baptism were per-
secuted and often killed for their testimony. But says Paul,
if there be no resurrection, then why suffer for a cause which
is not real after all and based only upon supposition. That
this seems to be the sense is indicated by the next verse:

And why stand we in jeopardy every hour? (I Corinthians
15:30).

Paul was in constant danger of violence and even of death
because of his faith in the death and the resurrection of Christ.
But if his faith were based on a mistake and an error and a
lie, then why should he suffer for it and why should he be
baptized as a public testimony of faith in something which was
not real. To declare oneself as a believer in Paul's day,
especially by being baptized, subjected such a one to the
hatred of the infidels. Today we are told that in heathen
lands the final step which is considered to be intolerable, is
the step of professing publicly ones faith in the Lord Jesus
by baptism. Yea, Paul could say, "I die daily."

Paul had faced death many times for his faith. He had
even been put in the arena to be fed to the wild beasts. This
is implied in verse 32:

If after the manner of men I have fought with beasts at
Ephesus, what advantageth it me, if the dead rise not? Let
us eat and drink; for tomorrow we die (I Corinthians 15:32).

What is the use of suffering for the cause of Christ if
there is nothing beyond, and this life is the end of everything. Whether Paul refers here to literal combat with wild
beasts in the arena at Ephesus, or refers to his human per-
secutors does not alter his argument. Why submit to all this

torture and sacrifice for the sake of Christ if our faith in the resurrection and the future life is all in vain. Then away with our profession; "let us eat and drink; for tomorrow we die."

But the apostle Paul, of course, knew better. He had met the risen Christ. He had seen Him and experienced His daily presence with him and therefore could say:

> For I reckon that the sufferings of this present time are not worthy to be compared with the glory which shall be revealed in us (Romans 8:18).

And in Philippians 3 we hear him say:

> But what things were gain to me, those I counted loss for Christ.
>
> Yea doubtless, and I count all things but loss for the excellency of the knowledge of Christ Jesus my Lord: for whom I have suffered the loss of all things, and do count them but dung, that I may win Christ,
>
> And be found in him, not having mine own righteousness, which is of the law, but that which is through the faith of Christ, the righteousness which is of God by faith:
>
> That I may know him, and the power of his resurrection, and the fellowship of his sufferings, being made conformable unto his death;
>
> If by any means I might attain unto the resurrection of the dead (Philippians 3:7-11).

Yes, indeed, says Paul, there is a life after death, which will make all of our suffering seem like nothing here below. There is an eternity ahead, a long, long eternity either with Christ, or in outer darkness. And this destiny depends on the resurrection of the Lord Jesus Christ. Those who believe the Gospel that Christ died and rose again will spend eternity in ineffable bliss. Those who reject Him will hear their doom:

> Depart from me, ye cursed, into everlasting fire, prepared for the devil and his angels (Matthew 25:41).

What will your destiny be? You can settle it right this moment by coming to Christ and believing the Gospel that

> . . . Christ died for our sins according to the scriptures;
>
> And that he was buried, and that he rose again the third day according to the scriptures (I Corinthians 15:3, 4).

*Chapter Twenty-seven*

# OUR RESURRECTION BODIES

WHAT will our resurrection bodies be like when they are finally raised from the dead at Jesus' coming? Will our new bodies resemble our old bodies which were placed in the grave? Will these bodies bear personally the characteristics they had here while upon the earth? Will we be able to recognize and know one another in heaven? These and many other questions are constantly being asked by our listeners. But they are not new questions at all, for the believers were already asking the same questions in Paul's day.

In I Corinthians 15, the great resurrection chapter of the Bible, Paul seeks to answer some of these problems. We read, therefore, in verse 35:

> But some man will say, How are the dead raised up? and with what body do they come? (I Corinthians 15:35).

The question was, How are the dead raised? Or rather, In what form will they appear at the resurrection day. What will their bodies be like? Listen now to the answer of Paul:

> Thou fool, that which thou sowest is not quickened, except it die:
>
> And that which thou sowest, thou sowest not that body that shall be, but bare grain, it may chance of wheat, or of some other grain.
>
> But God giveth it a body as it hath pleased him, and to every seed his own body (I Corinthians 15:36-38).

Paul resorts to the figure of a planted seed of wheat which is placed in the ground. The original kernel which is planted dies and rots away, but it results in a new crop of grains, all of them just like the one which was planted. Each seed planted will spring up with new seed which will resemble in every way that which was sown. To be sure there have been new elements added, and the old seed itself has perished and wasted away, but yet the new seed which comes forth out of the death of the old is similar in every respect to that which was planted. Our body, therefore, in the resurrection will resemble our present body (without the infirmities and blemishes and faults which it has here below). We will not all look alike in heaven, but we will be as different in appearance as we are here below. We will still retain our individuality and our personality. In the resurrection we do not lose our distinctive personality or identity. We will all have perfect bodies, yet different in appearance and, therefore, recognizable even more so than here below. An illustration follows in verse 39:

> All flesh is not the same flesh: but there is one kind of flesh of men, another flesh of beasts, another of fishes, and another of birds.
>
> There are also celestial bodies, and bodies terrestrial: but the glory of the celestial is one, and the glory of the terrestrial is another.
>
> There is one glory of the sun, and another glory of the moon, and another glory of the stars; for one star differeth from another star in glory.
>
> So also is the resurrection of the dead (I Corinthians 15: 39-42a).

As there are differences among things on earth, and among the heavenly bodies, the sun and the moon and the stars in the heavens, so will there be differences in the appearance of the resurrected bodies of the saints about which Paul is talking. As we are able to recognize different stars by their physical characteristics, so too we will be able to recognize one another in heaven by these same personal differences. But in certain other ways our bodies will be infinitely different from our natural bodies, and so Paul continues:

> It is sown in corruption; it is raised in incorruption:

> It is sown in dishonour; it is raised in glory: it is sown in weakness; it is raised in power:
>
> It is sown a natural body; it is raised a spiritual body. There is a natural body, and there is a spiritual body (I Corinthians 15:42b-44).

While it is true that we will bear the likeness of our bodies here, there will be, however, a great difference, for our resurrection bodies will be:

1. Incorruptible bodies. They shall never know sickness, pain, never grow old and never have to die. Sown in corruption but raised in incorruption.

2. They will be bodies of honor. Paul says that these natural bodies are sown in dishonor. Yes indeed, what a dishonorable testimony the death of these bodies becomes, to have to admit that we were so sinfully corrupt that even these bodies must submit to death and can never as such inhabit the kingdom of heaven, but we shall be raised again in glory.

3. These bodies will be powerful bodies, not subject to weakness and weariness, for there we shall never tire; our spiritual bodies will not need replenishing or even sleep, and hence, there will be no need for night.

4. These resurrection bodies will be spiritual bodies. While visible and tangible they will not be subject to the laws of nature as our bodies are today, but will be subject only to the laws of the spirit. Our natural bodies are subject to the limiting laws which hem us in here below, but our spiritual bodies will be able to rise above the laws of time and of space. They will be able to travel great distances in the winking of an eye. They will be able to pass through closed doors.

All this is implied in the next verse:

> And so it is written, The first man Adam was made a living soul; the last Adam was made a quickening spirit.
>
> The first man is of the earth, earthy: the second man is the Lord from heaven.

As is the earthy, such are they also that are earthy: and as is the heavenly, such are they also that are heavenly.

And as we have borne the image of the earthy, we shall also bear the image of the heavenly (I Corinthians 15:45, 47-49).

Here, then, we have the final answer. We receive our natural bodies from Adam, and therefore they are like Adam's physical body. But our resurrection bodies will be like the resurrection body of the Lord Jesus Christ Himself, for says the Scripture:

We shall also bear the image of the heavenly (I Corinthians 15:49b).

The body of our Lord Jesus Christ after His resurrection was a spiritual body. But notice some things about this spiritual body:

1. It was a recognizable body. It bore the print of the nails, and the wounds in His side. Mary recognized Jesus by His voice when He said, "Mary" (John 20:16). We are told that the reason the disciples did not recognize Him was that their eyes were "holden," not because the Lord was not easily recognized (Luke 24:16, Luke 24:31).

2. Jesus' body could move from one place to another in a moment of time, and disappear at will. (Luke 24:31). He could ascend straight upward (Acts 1:9). He could enter a room where the doors were locked (John 20:19).

3. We shall not need food, but we will be able to partake of it at will. The Bible says, "They shall hunger no more neither shall they thirst any more" (Revelation 7). Yet we shall be able to eat, for Jesus proved that it was indeed He who had risen from the grave by eating before the eyes of His disciples (Luke 24:42).

4. Our bodies, therefore, will be like His glorified body. In Philippians 3:20 we read:

For our conversation is in heaven; from whence also we look for the Saviour, the Lord Jesus Christ:

Who shall change our vile body, that it may be fashioned like unto *his glorious body* (Philippians 3:20, 21a).

## WHEN WILL IT HAPPEN?

And this, of course, brings us to the final section of this great fifteenth chapter of I Corinthians on the resurrection. We are now told exactly when this resurrection will happen:

Behold, I show you a mystery; We shall not all sleep, but we shall all be changed,

In a moment, in the twinkling of an eye, at the last trump: for the trumpet shall sound, and the dead shall be raised incorruptible, and we shall be changed (I Corinthians 15:51, 52).

This is the glorious metamorphosis which will take place at Jesus' return for His Church. When this occurs, all the dead in Christ shall rise first, and then those who are still alive at that particular time will be suddenly transfigured and will exchange their mortal bodies for immortal, incorruptible, glorified bodies. That is the order. First the dead in Christ shall be raised, then the living believers shall be changed, and then together they shall rise to meet the Lord in the air. You will notice from these passages that the dead are always mentioned first, for Paul says:

For this corruptible [the dead] must put on incorruption, and this mortal [the living believers] must put on immortality (I Corinthians 15:53).

Dead bodies are corruptible, living bodies are not corruptible, but mortal (subject to death). This, then, is the order: first the corrupting dead bodies will be raised from the grave, then the mortal living bodies will be changed.

But all of this applies only to the resurrection of the saved, those who have died in the faith of the Lord Jesus. What the condition of the bodies of the lost will be in the last and final resurrection, the Bible nowhere tells us clearly. They will be raised, but no hint is given in the Bible that they will be any different from the bodies in which the lost lived and died. The bodies of the lost at the resurrection will not be glorified bodies. They will not be honorable bodies. They evidently will not be free from the pains and the ills and the sufferings of these bodies in this world and in this life. There the drunkard will thirst forever without a drop of drink. There they will hunger but never be satisfied. The harlot will burn, but never be gratified. The Bible tells us concerning these in Revelation:

> But the fearful, and unbelieving, and the abominable, and murderers, and whoremongers, and sorcerers, and idolaters, and all liars, shall have their part in the lake which burneth with fire and brimstone: which is the second death (Rev. 21:8).

No, my friend, death does not end all. All men will some day be raised from the dead, some to everlasting life and some to everlasting damnation. And so the important question which faces each one is, What will be YOUR portion in that day. It will depend entirely upon your choice right here and right now. If you will receive Christ as Saviour, then you will live with Him forever in indescribable bliss. If you reject Him here and now, you are thereby choosing your own damnation, for says our Lord:

> He that believeth on him is not condemned: but he that believeth not is condemned already, because he hath not believed in the name of the only begotten Son of God.
>
> And this is the condemnation, that light is come into the world, and men loved darkness rather than light, because their deeds were evil (John 3:18, 19).

To us who believe, the entire future is bright, and we dread not what lies ahead, when we listen to the promises of God which cannot fail:

> And God shall wipe away all tears from their eyes; and there shall be no more death, neither sorrow, nor crying, neither shall there be any more pain: for the former things are passed away (Revelation 21:4).

Surely all of this causes us to cry out from a heart of gratitude and longing, "Even so come, Lord Jesus."

*Chapter Twenty-eight*

# THE STING OF DEATH

> Behold, I show you a mystery; We shall not all sleep, but we shall all be changed,
>
> In a moment, in the twinkling of an eye, at the last trump: for the trumpet shall sound, and the dead shall be raised incorruptible, and we shall be changed.
>
> For this corruptible must put on incorruption, and this mortal must put on immortality.
>
> So when this corruptible shall have put on incorruption, and this mortal shall have put on immortality, then shall be brought to pass the saying that is written, Death is swallowed up in victory (I Corinthians 15:51-54).

DEATH is the enemy of man. It is an enemy to be dreaded, for death is the result of sin. There is no such thing as a natural death. All death is unnatural, for God created man to live and not to die. But sin entered the human race and death by sin, and man naturally dreads death and will give all that he has in order to retain his life.

But since sin is the cause of death, it is also the cause of man's dread of death. Therefore, the fear of death can only be removed by removing its cause, namely *sin*. For this reason the believer whose sins have been carried by the Saviour need not dread death, for it becomes then only a change of residence from this sinful earth with all of its suffering, to the bliss and the joys of an eternal heaven. And then later, at the resurrection, we shall receive new resurrection bodies, painless, sinless, deathless bodies to enjoy God's new heaven and new earth forever and forever without a sigh or a moan or a tear. That is what Paul means in our Scripture:

186

Death is swallowed up in victory (I Corinthians 15:54b).
And then he continues:

O death, where is thy sting? O grave, where is thy victory?
The sting of death is sin; and the strength of sin is the law.
But thanks be to God, which giveth us the victory through
our Lord Jesus Christ (I Cor. 15:55-57).

## COMPLETE VICTORY

This is indeed a shout of victory. Paul could stand up before his enemy, death, and shout in his face:

O death, where is thy sting? O grave, where is thy victory?
(I Corinthians 15:55).

And then he gives the answer for it. The sting of death is gone. Death is here represented as a hornet or a bee. But its stinger has been removed so that it has become harmless. Now the sting of death is sin, according to the words of Paul. It is because of sin that we dread death. To die and stand before God with sin upon us unatoned and unforgiven is a terrible prospect which causes fear and trembling in the heart of man. It will mean eternal damnation, and, therefore, death for unbelievers means the passing into the place of outer darkness and condemnation forever and ever. To face God at death without Christ our sinbearer, is an awful, terrible, fearful prospect. And only the taking care of the sting of death, which is sin, can take away this fear.

## STING IS GONE

But how different for the believer all this becomes. His sin has been taken care of, paid for, atoned for, forgiven and forgotten. He is complete in Christ, and death means only a "going home" without fear of judgment for sin. His sins are gone, and death has lost its sting forever. Let us remember, therefore, that the sting of death is *sin,* and when sin is removed, the sting is taken care of entirely.

Let me illustrate. Some years ago I was greatly interested in the keeping of bees, not so much for the profit they produced as the unending source of joy and education they afforded me. Many, many were the precious lessons I learned from the little busy bodies. Many were the illustrations of sublime spiritual truths they were able to teach me. One thing I learned was that a worker bee can sting *only once* in a lifetime. Its needle-sharp stinger is equipped with little barbs all along its sides like a porcupine quill, so that when the stinger is inserted it goes in to stay, and causes the death of the bee. The stinger of a bee, once it has entered the flesh, cannot be withdrawn, because of these barbs. The only way, therefore, that the bee can free itself is to tear away from the stinger, leaving it behind in the victim whom it has attacked. It is now a bee without a sting. It is harmless. It can still buzz, but it cannot sting.

One cloudy day I walked with my two sons, Richard and Marvin, through the orchard among the bee hives. The boys were just little lads, and in some way irritated the bees. One of the bees made straight for Richard's head, and before he could do a thing about it, it sunk its sting into his flesh above his eye. With a howl of pain he brushed it away, only to have it dart directly at Marvin's head. At this Marvin screamed (though unhurt) at the top of his voice, and falling to the ground, hid his face in the grass. But I raised him up and said, "Listen, that bee cannot hurt you, it can only scare you." And then I took him over to Richard, still crying, and showed him the little dark speck, still deeply imbedded in the flesh of his brother. "There is the bee sting. He left it in your brother and now it is harmless as far as you are concerned. It can still alarm you with its buzzing and scare you almost to death, but it has no power to sting any more and soon it will die."

### SERMON IN THE ORCHARD

And there in the orchard I had the precious privilege of preaching a sermon to my two sons. The sting of death is sin, and is compared to the sting of a bee. But our Elder Brother, Jesus, took our sin upon Himself and was, as it were, stung to death by our sin. Now the sting of death is gone, for He "bare our sins in his own body on the tree, that we, being dead to sins, might live unto righteousness" (I Peter 2:24).

The sting of death, therefore, is gone. Death can still "buzz" the believer and scare him almost out of his wits, but thank God it is harmless to injure us in any way. Death can only open the door for us to heaven.

The law demanded our death. The law said:

The soul that sinneth, it shall die (Ezekiel 18:4b).

And so Paul says (verse 56):

The strength of sin is the law (I Corinthians 15:56b).

But Christ our Saviour came and fulfilled the law, met all of its demands, paid its full penalty, and now we are saved by grace, free from the law and its condemnation. Now we can understand Paul's exultant cry of victory:

O death, where is thy sting? O grave, where is thy victory?
The sting of death is sin; and the strength of sin is the law.
But thanks be to God, which giveth us the victory through our Lord Jesus Christ (I Corinthians 15:55, 57).

How wonderful, therefore, it is to know that when this life is over, we have an eternity of bliss ahead because sin cannot touch us anymore. The best is yet to come and we can say with Paul in verses 57 and 58:

But thanks be to God, which giveth us the victory through our Lord Jesus Christ.
Therefore, my beloved brethren, be ye steadfast, unmovable, always abounding in the work of the Lord, forasmuch as ye know that your labor is not in vain in the Lord (I Corinthians 15:57, 58).

## THE COLLECTION

We come now to the closing chapter of I Corinthians, and it begins rather abruptly on an entirely different note:

Now concerning the collection for the saints, as I have given order to the churches of Galatia, even so do ye.
Upon the first day of the week let every one of you lay by him in store, as God hath prospered him, that there be no gatherings [collections] when I come (I Corinthians 16:1, 2).

Paul waited until the very last before he mentioned the matter of money. Evidently Paul hated the mention of collections and would much rather not have mentioned them àt all, but he had no alternative. He did not want any collections when he came to them. He did not desire that the services should be interrupted for the taking of offerings. And to be sure, there need be no collections if all of God's people would heed Paul's instruction in these two verses. One of the saddest commentaries on the ignorance of God's Word among believers is the need of all the different drives and schemes and pleas for money to keep God's work going. All kinds of begging and schemes and gadgets and worthless trinkets are held out as bait to separate God's people from their money. One of the greatest reproaches upon modern-day evangelism and Bible conferences is the terrific pressure for money and the embarrassing amount of time consumed in the raising of funds for the campaign. It is my firm conviction that if we are doing God's work, and faithfully, prayerfully giving out the Word, and teaching believers the Bible order of giving, that we need never worry about finances. God will take care of His own. Notice, therefore, Paul's instructions for Scriptural giving:

1. It must be out of a heart of love first of all. It must not be a legal procedure. This collection was for the poor saints at Jerusalem and must be motivated by love alone. It was not for ornate buildings and edifices, but for the profit of others.

2. It must be systematic. Upon the first day of the week they were to "lay by" their offering to the Lord. Giving must not be haphazard, but regular and systematic. The regular supporters of the Gospel are the people who keep the work going, not the "hit and miss, now and then" spasmodic givers, of whom there are so many.

3. It is a personal responsibility. "Let *every one* of you lay by him in store." No setting up of a budget and assessing the members, or squeezing and pressing to meet our man-

made requirements. No need of committees and teams to raise the money needed for the work of the Lord.

4. Next notice that it must be proportionate. There is nothing here about tithing at all. Not a single word about a tenth, but instead, "as God hath prospered him." Some folks could give 90 percent of their income and still have a hundred times more left for themselves than some poor person who gave one-tenth. The poor widow's mite counts more with God than the large sums of others whose gifts are larger in amount but are smaller in proportion.

If these simple instructions were followed, there would be enough and more for all the needs of the work of the Lord's people. If all the money spent for promotional schemes and gadgets to raise more money could be used for the Gospel, much of the reproach caused by too many present-day methods would be removed. I repeat, I firmly believe that if we are faithful in preaching the Word that God Himself will take care of us.

With this we conclude our series of messages on I Corinthians. The balance of chapter 16 contains personal greetings and instructions to the church. They are of real importance, but we have covered the main portions of the book and suggest a careful reading of the rest of the chapter for your own devotions. We close, therefore with verse 22:

> If any man love not the Lord Jesus Christ, let him be Anathema Maranatha (I Corinthians 16:22).

It is the final serious warning of the apostle Paul to this carnal and worldly church. "Anathema" means accursed. All who reject God's Word shall be accursed. And then follows the word "Maranatha!" "Maranatha" means "our Lord Cometh." This is an admonition not only to the sinner, but especially to the people of God to remind them that the coming of the Lord is drawing nigh, when we shall all have to give an account and stand before the judgment seat of Christ. Yes, indeed, our Lord cometh. Even though the

Church has waited for all of these centuries, we know that the Day of the Lord will come, and then we shall receive the rewards which we have laid up by faithful service and by heeding the admonitions of the Lord as so wonderfully given by Paul.

And then the question is, What will be your destiny? One of these days, it will all be over and the time of opportunity and grace will come to an end. Eternity lies ahead, a long endless eternity. What we do with the Lord Jesus Christ will determine our destiny forever, either in heaven or in the place of the lost. May the Lord grant us grace to take these warnings and admonitions and instructions seriously and to remember the words:

> The foundation of God standeth sure, having this seal, The Lord knoweth them that are his. And, Let every one that nameth the name of Christ depart from iniquity (II Timothy 2:19).

MARANATHA